Glad
You
Asked

Scriptural
Answers
for Our
Times

Glad You Asked

Scriptural Answers for Our Times

John H. Hampsch, C.M.F.

Our Sunday Visitor Publishing Division
Our Sunday Visitor, Inc.
Huntington, Indiana 46750

466

CONTENTS

PREFACE

"Why do you always answer a question by asking another one?" a wife inquired of her husband.

"Do I?" was the inevitable response.

Even God sometimes answers questions by asking other questions, as he did with Job, who questioned him about the suffering of innocent persons (Job, 38:1 and 42:4). But more often, the Lord answers questions with a non-question statement that triggers further questions; thus, answering Philip's question about the revelation of the Father (Jn. 14:8) led to Jude's question about Jesus' own self-revelation (v. 22).

In any inquiry, especially a religious one, questions tend to become concatenated, linked together; the answer to one question often triggers another question. Like eating peanuts one at a time, it's often difficult to curtail the sequence. Follow-up questions, either by way of challenge or natural inquisitiveness, often spawn a lively discussion, with surprisingly profound insights, especially if the questioner has a probing mind, one not easily satisfied with superficial answers.

Recognizing this dynamic in human discourse, the Athenian philosopher Socrates scientized it into what has come to be known as the Socratic method, sometimes also called the "heuristic" method (from the Greek word *heuriskein*, meaning to discover). It consists of an attempt to discover truth by questioning each answer to a previous question, in logical, not haphazard sequence. Having stood the test of twenty-four centuries, it is still recognized as perhaps the most effective form of pedagogical disquisition, and today it is used in many computerized teaching programs.

In this book of questions and answers on religious, moral, ethical, and spiritual issues, the heuristic method is employed, not directly, but only indirectly by anticipating in each answer further challenging questions or objections, and forestalling them by expanding the answers. This, hopefully, makes for a tight, well-structured, and relatively complete body of knowledge on each subject matter dealt with. If this work requires an apologia for its existence amidst a plethora of question-and-answer books flooding the market today, it would be, I feel, mainly because of this implicit use of the heuristic method.

A second rationale for the book is that, unlike many such books, it limits itself primarily to questions that have a practical rather than speculative import, whether for one's own personal information or to make the reader better equipped to engage in religious discussions with others. It doesn't attempt to deal with narrow issues like liturgical niceties, pious devotions, or matters of less than universal interest.

A third rationale for the book is that it attempts to provide a substantial scriptural basis for each response in greater detail than is found in most books of this genre. Among other advantages, this enables the book to be used more effectively in ecumenical study clubs, etc.

Although the presentation is basically from the Catholic perspective, the non-Catholic reader will not feel uncomfortable with the book, both because of the nondenominational nature of most of the questions themselves, and because of the scriptural corroboration of the material presented. Further, truth-hungry non-Catholics will welcome those few sections that offer clarification of Catholic teachings, often misconstrued or misunderstood by Catholics and non-Catholics alike.

It is hoped that this book will serve to remind us that questions play a vital role in our lives as Christian believers; they make us think about truths we might otherwise accept blindly. Asking questions and questioning answers is not an affront to God. Rather, it makes us aware of our dependence on him who is the way, the Truth and the Life — the one who has all the answers to our questions.

Yet it is also good to remind ourselves that sometimes God chooses not to share those answers with us completely, by leaving them in the realm of mystery. Mystery, in theology, is defined as a revealed truth that we do not *fully* understand (like the mystery of the three Persons in one God, or the timing of the end of the world). If there were no mysteries, we would have the very omniscience of God himself. Accepting our less-than-God limitation is an act of humility, while accepting truth without proof (other than God's revelation) is an act of faith.

As truth-seekers, we need then to be reminded that questions are to be answered, while mysteries are to be lived. Questions are rope knots we strive to untangle, while mysteries are ropes we hang onto like mountain climbers, knowing that the ropes are well anchored with pitons in the rock.

Job had to learn where questions end and mystery begins. Confronted by the Lord when his questions about suffering led him across the threshold of mystery, as God began to counter-question him, Job then backpedaled: "Surely I spoke of things I did not understand, things too wonderful for me to know. . . . Therefore I repent in dust and ashes" (Job 42: 3-6).

This book is designed to explore some questions as far as theology will guide us, but also to delineate the God-set limits of human knowledge of divine truths, so that our questioning doesn't echo the querulousness of Job, tempting us to strive rashly to cross that unbridgeable chasm into the sacred realm of mystery.

Subsequent volumes of the "Glad You Asked" series are currently projected, mainly because of the insistent encouragement of the readers of *The SCRC Vision*, a Los Angeles-based monthly periodical in which this material was first published as a regular column titled the same as this book. Our thanks to the publishers of *The Vision* for reprint rights, and to the readers of that column who submitted the questions.

One suggestion for the casual or non-methodical reader: Topics of preferential interest can be winnowed out by a cursory glance at the index, rather than by reading each question.

It is the prayer of the author that this modest treatise will leave its readers better informed, more secure in their belief in Christian truths, and more aware of the scriptural basis for those beliefs.

John H. Hampsch, C.M.F.
Claretian Tape Ministry
Los Angeles, California

Angels, Saints, and Heaven

What are angels?

Angels are referred to in Scripture more than 300 times. In general, angels are ministering spirits (Heb. 1:14), and as the Greek word for angel (*angelos*) signifies, their primary ministerial role is acting as messengers (2:2).

God's myriads of angels, "mighty ones who do his bidding" (Ps. 103:20), are beings with a superlative intellect and incredible power. Of the nine angelic "choirs" or orders, referred to in various places in Scripture, our guardians belong to the order closest to the human level. As angels, they are lower than archangels, virtues, powers, principalities, dominations, thrones, cherubim and seraphim. Yet their abilities and intelligence and holiness are inconceivably greater than ours. Having such an angelic companion is better than having super-holy Superman as our private intercessor, servant, bodyguard, and friend.

Is there a guardian angel for every person?

Yes, all do indeed have a personal guardian angel. And the full acknowledgment and realization of that truth should utterly transform the life of anyone, just as the many angelic apparitions mentioned in the Bible transformed the lives of those who saw them. Either seeing or truly believing that you have the awesome privilege of a personally assigned guardian angel would convince you, for instance, that there is no such thing as solitary confinement; the loneliest widow in the world would no longer languish in loneliness or self-pity; those tempted to lust would find it unthinkable to sin in the presence of their heavenly companion; those tempted to discouragement or despair would be reinvigorated by the radiant presence of their angel companion, etc.

For those angels assigned to us individually as guardian angels, their main function seems to be that of guarding and protecting us: "He will command his angels . . . to *guard* you in all your ways, . . . so you will not strike your foot. . ." etc. (Ps. 91:11-12).

The teaching about the existence of personal *guardian angels* (as distinguished from teachings about angels in general) is a doctrine of the Church classed as *proxima fidei*, that is, as a consistent and scripturally supported teaching that is affirmed by theological luminaries such as St. Jerome and St. Thomas Aquinas (whose extensive writings on angels earned him the title "Angelic Doctor").

There is a class of evil spirits (fallen angels) known as "familiar spirits" (referred to in Leviticus, Deuteronomy, 1 Samuel, 2 Kings, 1 and 2 Chronicles and Isaiah), so called because they become familiar with our weaknesses so as to attack us in those areas. Likewise, there is a class of holy angels, at least one of which is assigned by God to each human; they too become familiar with our weaknesses and strengths, and are commissioned by God to protect us, to inspire us, to pray for us, to encourage and support us in trials, etc. *All* holy angels are "ministering spirits sent to serve" (Heb. 1:14), but those ministering spirits assigned as special protectors of individual humans are those traditionally called guardian angels.

Do all have guardian angels, or only righteous persons? St. Jerome and St. Basil held that serious sin drives away one's guardian angel, leaving sinners vulnerable to spiritual and perhaps even physical hurt in life's spiritual warfare. Although this is somewhat conjectural, and *perhaps* contrary to Jesus' remarks about God's indiscriminate beneficence to saint and sinner alike (Mt. 5:45), still there may be some basis for the conjecture. God does withdraw many favors from those who disobey him (Deut. 28:15-68). Psalm 91 promises angelic protection "*if* you make the Most High your dwelling" (verse 9); it refers to God-lovers: "because he loves me . . . I will rescue him" (verse 14). "The angel of the Lord encamps around *those who fear* (reverence) *him*" (Ps. 34:8). And Scripture clearly states that angels are "sent to serve those who will inherit salvation" (Heb. 1:14). Although it is possible that God may send angels to protect those who will not inherit salvation, yet there is no scriptural indication that he does so.

Will the resurrected bodies of the saved be just like the resurrected body of Christ?

The resurrected bodies of the elect will be not just "spiritualized" (1 Cor. 15:44), with physical integrity and immortality, like those of the damned, but, unlike the damned, they will be also "glorified" (Col. 3:4) like the resurrected body of Jesus (Phil. 3:21). Jesus, by his resurrection and ascension, and Mary, by bodily Assumption into heaven, have both had a "premature rapture" as it were, and therefore have glorified bodies now, unlike the other saints in heaven who are disembodied souls at this time, awaiting the resurrection of their body on the last day. These saints, in their occasional apparition on earth, do not present themselves in a glorified body; their apparition is merely a "projected" presence, like that of angels in human disguise (Heb. 13:2), made visible by a divine miraculous intervention. An exception would be Elijah at the transfiguration apparition (with Jesus and Moses); Elijah is not a disembodied soul, for he never died, but was transported bodily to heaven (2 Kings 2:11-12).

The glorified body will have four characteristics of the risen Christ. The first is effulgent beauty or radiance ("clarity" is the technical term) manifested by Jesus at his pre-resurrection transfiguration when "his face shone like the sun" (Mt. 17:2) and "his clothes became dazzling white" (Mk. 9:3). "The righteous will shine like the sun in the kingdom of their Father" (Mt. 13:43; see Wis. 3:7). "As star differs from star in splendor" (1 Cor. 15:41) the blessed will manifest various degrees of this quality, and they can suspend it at will, says Aquinas (e.g., as Jesus did to remain incognito at Emmaus).

The second characteristic of the glorified body is "subtlety," that is, the ability to interpenetrate matter, as the risen Jesus did when he walked through the locked door (Jn. 20:19). Notwithstanding this ability to compenetrate matter, the glorified body is palpable — that is, it can be felt normally (as the body of the Virgin Mary was touched and felt, it is claimed, by the visionaries at Medjugorje). The risen Jesus invited the test of palpability of his glorified body: "Touch me and see; a ghost does not have flesh and bones, as you see I have" (Lk. 24:39). Thus subtlety, like effulgence (radiance), says St. Thomas, can be suspended at will, so that the body can be made palpable and thus touched and felt normally by another, as in an embrace, fondling, etc.

The third characteristic of the glorified bodies of the elect will be "agility" — the ability to move effortlessly and with extreme rapidity from place to place. "They will soar on wings like eagles; they will run and not grow weary" (Is. 40:31). "They shall run to and fro like sparks" (Wis. 3:7). This agility is a dimension of the glorified body's power (1 Cor. 15:43), which, says St. Thomas, is an overflow of the soul's power.

Jesus manifested this agility in his ascension (Acts 1:9), when he "leapfrogged" ahead of his disciples to Galilee (Mt. 28: 7-10), and when he "disappeared" from the disciples at Emmaus (Lk. 24:31). We shall first manifest it at the resurrection of our bodies when we are "caught up" (1 Thess. 4:17) — that is, "raptured" (see Jn. 5:29).

The fourth characteristic of the glorified body — of special interest to those who are afflicted in any way — is "impassibility"; that is, total freedom from physical, emotional or spiritual suffering, hardship, and sorrow. "Never again will they hunger . . . never again thirst . . . God will wipe away every tear from their eyes" (Rev. 7:16-17). "There will be no more death or mourning or crying or pain" (21:4). "The sovereign Lord will take away the tears from all faces; he will remove disgrace" (Is. 25:8). "Everlasting joy will crown their heads. Gladness will overtake them, and sorrow and sighing will flee away" (35:10; 51:11). Fear, deformities, deafness, wrinkles, overweight, baldness, depression, loneliness, anxiety, insecurity, addictions, etc. will not exist in heaven.

What will it be like to have a resurrected body at the end of time?

This question was anticipated by St. Paul. After a discourse on the resurrection of the body, he launches into more detail by citing your question: "Someone may ask, 'How are the dead raised? With what kind of body will they come?' " (1 Cor. 15:35). His answer describes not just the resurrection of the dead bodies but also the dramatic instantaneous transformation of the bodies still living when Jesus comes again (see 1 Thess. 4:15-17). "Listen, I tell you a mystery: We will not all die, but we will all be changed — in a flash, in the twinkling of an eye, at the last trumpet. The trumpet will sound, the dead will be raised imperishable, and we [who are still living] will be changed" (1 Cor. 15:51-52).

One of the best things about heaven and one of the worst things about hell will be the resurrected bodies we will receive on the last day. Persons living on earth at that time, whether they are to be saved or damned, will receive new imperishable bodies, which will share in the soul's reward or punishment for all eternity. Jesus clearly states this in John 5:29, reiterating what Daniel had prophesied (Dan. 12:2; see also Is. 26:19-21). "When he [Jesus] appears, we shall be like him" (1 Jn. 3:2). Those already in heaven at that time will be much happier from that day on, and those already in hell will experience much more anguish from that day on, says St. Thomas Aquinas.

The new bodies of the damned, like those of the elect, will be imperishable (1 Cor. 15:52) — that is, indestructible; they cannot die (although the damned are "dead" to the life of grace). Both the saved and the reprobate will have bodies that are integral; i.e., any amputated or missing parts will be restored (see 2 Mac. 7:11 and 14:46). There will be no defective eyesight or arthritic deformities, etc. in either the saved or condemned persons. However, in the reprobate, defects resulting from the nature of the body itself, such as fatigue, pain sensitivity, etc., will be present to instrument their punishment (partially). Their features will appear horribly ugly, but not with any deformity that would violate the due proportion of parts to the whole, surmises St. Thomas (St. Augustine had doubts about this conjecture).

In our weariness "we groan, longing to be clothed with our heavenly dwelling" (2 Cor. 5:2). The exciting revelation of what awaits us in our glorified body should be a stimulus for hope. It is thrilling to know that "by the power that enables him to bring everything under his control, he will transform our lowly bodies so they will be like his own glorious body" (Phil. 3:21). The prospect of it is intoxicating!

Why does the concept of purgatory seem to be neglected now?

Some Catholic writers and preachers downplay the emphasis on the doctrine of purgatory (perhaps as a diluted attempt to be ecumenical). Yet, ironically, the doctrine of purgatory itself is becoming accepted by more and more non-Catholic theologians, especially in Germany, Denmark, and England. These are returning to the concept of purgatory as a "post-death purification," a teaching held by the Jews from the time of Captivity, six centuries before Christ.

These non-Catholic theologians are also coming to approve intercessory prayer for the dead commonly practiced a century before Christ (2 Maccabees 12:43-46) and commonly accepted by Jesus' fellow Jews in his day, as Josephus wrote in A.D. 70 (the "Kaddish," or Jewish prayer for the dead, used from the first century, appeared to be based on Malachi 4:3 and Psalm 49:14-15). Perhaps it was in that context that St. Paul prayed for the deceased Onesiphorus (2 Tim. 1:16-18).

A Vatican II decree, *Gaudium et Spes* (which never used the word "punishment" but only "purification" when speaking of purgatory) said that our faith gives us the power to be united with our beloved dead (Eph. 3:15), but only in and through Christ (Rom. 14:9), as parts of his Mystical Body (Eph.4:1-6). Article 51 urges that the abusive presentation of this doctrine should be discontinued and corrected. Purgatory is not to be regarded as God's torture chamber.

What does the Church teach about the "end times"?

Catholic theology speaks of the "resurrection of the body," as in the Apostles' Creed — or "resurrection of the dead" as in the Nicene Creed. Of course, the living can't be "resurrected," but they will be changed by acquiring a "spiritual body" (1 Cor. 15:44); for heaven-bound persons this will be a glorified "resurrection body," like that of the risen Christ (1 Cor. 15:49; Rom. 8:11). This will happen in a flash — "in the twinkling of an eye, at the last trumpet," when "the dead will be raised imperishable, and we [the living] will be changed" (1 Cor. 15:52).

Twice Paul mentions that the resurrection of the dead will take place before the living are "changed" — probably immediately before. The resurrection of the dead will include both the saved and those to be damned, Jesus said (Jn. 5:29, quoting Dan. 12:2; see also Acts 24:15 and Rev. 20:13).

These dramatic events will take place at the time of the second coming of Christ (which, by the way, is mentioned directly or indirectly 318 times, in 22 of the 27 books of the

New Testament, and several hundred times in the Old Testament as the "Day of the Lord"). These same events of resurrection of the dead and change of the living will prepare both for a bodily presence through eternity in immortality (1 Cor. 15:53). These events will coincide with the second coming of Christ, and also with what has come to be called the "rapture."

The term "rapture" is derived from the classic reference in 1 Thess. 4:15-17: "According to the Lord's own word, we tell you that we who are still alive [at that future time] will certainly not precede those who have died. For the Lord himself will come down from heaven with a loud command, with the trumpet call of God, and the dead in Christ [righteous dead] will rise first. After that, we who are still alive and are left will be caught up ['raptured'] together with them in the clouds to meet the Lord in the air. And so we will be with the Lord forever."

The Greek word translated "caught up" in verse 17 is *harpazo*, which means to be "snatched away." The Latin equivalent to *harpazo*, used by St. Jerome in his translation into the official Catholic Latin Vulgate edition of the bible, is *raptus*, which is the past participle of the verb *rapio*. From this Latin word we get our English word "rapture." Hence the teaching about the "rapture." is not alien to Catholic doctrine, even though the word "rapture" is not used in the English translations usually.

Regarding the timing of the "rapture" as it relates to the "Great Tribulation" (spoken of by Jesus in Mt. 24:21 and referred to in Rev. 7:14), there is a flourishing controversy, encompassing three major eschatological positions — none of which is condemned by the Catholic Church. They are the "Pre-tribulation" theory, the "Post-tribulation" theory, and the "Mid-tribulation" theory; the designations are almost self-evident for each position.

The "Pre-trib" position was first formulated by John Nelson Darby in 1833. It holds that the righteous people will be "raptured" out of the world *before* the expected seven-year tribulation, thus avoiding the wrath of God that will be poured out.

The "Post-trib" position, on the other hand, teaches that the faithful will remain on earth through the tribulation to be purged and disciplined, and "raptured" afterward. This position was commonly held in the earliest centuries of the Church. Some of the adherents of this position feel that righteous persons will be miraculously preserved from suffering while the rest of the world witnesses this divine protection of the "those who revere his name" (Mal. 4:1-3).

The "Mid-trib" position holds that believers will undergo the first half of the tribulation, but will be "raptured" out of the world before the second and more severe half (Dan. 9:27). Some of the adherents of this position hold that this mid-tribulation rapture will be only for the tribulation martyrs, not for other righteous persons (Rev. 20:4-5); this "rapture is thought to be the "first resurrection" (vs. 6), according to this point of view.

(Don't confuse this controversy with another controversy that has to do with a cognate subject, the "millennium" or "thousand years" of Christ's reign (Rev. 20:4). Not all of the positions regarding *that* issue are acceptable in Catholic theology. Although each of the three major theories about the timing of the "rapture" can be buttressed by biblical passages, you might find one more convincing that the others. But be cautious about labeling other positions unbiblical or heretical. The historical coexistence of differing positions should suggest that the weight of tradition does not necessarily lie with any one view in this matter, even within Catholic circles. But at least be aware that the so-called "rapture" itself is a biblical and Catholic teaching.

In eschatological matters like this, it would be good to take note of Jesus' response to the end-time queries of his disciples, as in the 13th chapter of Mark. He reminds them of what things will *not* be signs of the end: "take heed" is a phrase used four

19

times in this discourse (vss. 5, 9, 23, 33). It indicates that we should not focus primarily on seeking out a "crystal-ball" revelation of the future, but rather prepare to live out a full discipleship in the midst of a chaotic and confusing future crisis. In the midst of suffering in end-times (if we are to be part of those times), it will seem that the end will never come. But strive to be among those who will have "persevered and endured hardships for my name, and have not grown weary" (Rev. 2:3).

If Jesus is the only mediator between God and humanity, what good can be accomplished by praying for the intercession of saints?

You are right in saying that Jesus is the only mediator between God and humanity, as it says in 1 Tim. 2:5, Acts 4:12, and Heb. 7:25. However, in all these passages Jesus is specifically referred to as redemptive mediator; no mention is made of Jesus being the only prayer mediator — that is, intercessor. Only Jesus redeemed us — no one else. But others, either in heaven or on earth, can be mediators by way of prayer. This type of mediatorship or intercession is mentioned many times in both Old and New Testaments; for instance, 1 Kings 13:6; Ps. 106:23; Eph. 1:16, etc. Judas Maccabeus saw a vision of Onias, the deceased holy High Priest, praying for the Jewish nation. He was accompanied by a vision of Jeremiah offering prayers for the Jews and for Jerusalem (2 Mac. 15: 12-16). But even when others on earth or in heaven pray for us, their prayers still are channeled through the ultimate mediator, Jesus: "No one comes to the Father except through me" (Jn. 14:6).

Our non-Catholic friends often accuse us of "praying to the saints." It would be more accurate to say that we pray with the saints, or ask them to pray with and for us. When the word "pray" is used in the broad sense, praying can mean to address someone prayerfully, asking that person to pray for us, as we do in the Hail Mary: "pray for us sinners." That means we ask her to pray to God for us while we pray to God for ourselves. Thus Mary or any angel or saint can be a mediator of prayer (intercessory prayer), just as you and I can for others. As Mary used her intercessory power to entice Jesus to work his Cana miracle "before his time" (Jn. 2:4), that same intercessory power is now available to her in heaven. It is certainly not weaker but stronger than it was on earth, as implied in Heb. 11:40 and 12:1. In this way Paul "prayed" that his fellow Christians would pray for him (Eph 6, Col. 4, Rom. 15), and he prayed for others (Eph. 3; Col. 1, etc.).

How are Catholics supposed to regard angels and saints if we don't worship them?

Catholics are not taught to worship any creature, angels, saints, or even the Virgin Mary, for that would be a terrible sin against the first commandment of God commanding us to worship only him (Deuteronomy 6:13, quoted by Jesus in response to Satan's temptation: Mt. 4:10; Lk. 4:8; see also 1 Sam. 7:3). But veneration is not worship; honoring a person is not necessarily worshiping that person. We honor or venerate political heroes by having holidays in their honor (Washington, Lincoln, Martin Luther King), by naming streets after them, publishing stamps in their honor, etc., and no one objects; there is less reason to object to honoring religious heroes by naming cities after them (St. Paul, St. Louis, Santa Monica, Santa Barbara, etc.). But an even better way of honoring them is by imitating their virtues, which leads us closer to Christ, the supreme example (1 Pet. 2:21). This form of veneration is quite biblical, since Paul asks us to be imitators of him — but only to the extent that he is an imitator of Christ (1 Cor. 11:1). In fact, Paul asks us to imitate his behavior in no less than seven places in the New Testament. St. James in his epistle (5:10) tells us to imitate the prophets in our acceptance of persecution. Hence, honoring by imitation of virtue does not detract from God, but leads us to him. That's why many Protestant evangelists strive to imitate the prayerfulness and zeal of champions like John Wesley, or Finney, or other great Protestant luminaries. This is part of our fellowship with the saints, living or dead (Eph. 3:15). Hebrews 11 speaks of inspiring examples of faith, and 12:1 speaks of being "surrounded by such a great cloud of witnesses" that should inspire us.

St. John made the mistake of falling down to worship an angel (Rev. 19:10); the angel told him not to do it, but to worship God instead. Peter corrected Cornelius for a similar mistake (Acts 10:25-26). So the Bible, which commands veneration of humans and angels, also forbids worship of them. Vatican II reaffirmed this as a consistent Catholic teaching, in accordance with the Scripture.

The Bible

Does Scripture support Catholic belief in Mary's Assumption?

The Catholic dogma of Mary's bodily Assumption into heaven, like the dogma of her Immaculate Conception, is supported by Scripture, although not directly but only indirectly, and this in three ways:

First, negatively, by the absence in the Bible of anything contrary to this teaching. Obviously, this negative support by itself is not a compelling one, and looks for other reasons to supplement it.

Secondly, particular cases of bodily "assumption" into heaven (or "raptures" as some prefer to call them) are mentioned in the Bible, and therefore the phenomenon as applicable to Mary is not unprecedented in Scripture. Five times the Bible refers to the "assumption," body and soul, of either Enoch or Elijah into heaven (see 2 Kings 2:11; Gen. 5:24; Jude 1:14; Heb. 11:5; Sirach 44:16 and 49:16).

Thirdly, the Bible, in eight places, validates tradition itself as a viable form of revelation, and Mary's Assumption privilege is based on a strong tradition traceable back to the 400s A.D. Tradition in this sense is a consistent belief held by the People of God from ancient times. This form of tradition is not merely *human* tradition, such as cultural or unwarranted disciplinary practices like those that Jesus condemned in Mt. 15:3 and 6, Mk. 7:8 and 13, and Paul condemned in Col. 2:8. The Bible states that God-authorized tradition is an acceptable form of revealed truth (serving Scripture, not replacing or dominating it, as Vatican II pointed out). The Bible tells us to "hold fast to the *traditions* that have been handed down to you, whether by word of mouth or by writing" (2 Thess. 2:15).

Other biblical references to tradition as a source of revelation include: 2 Tim. 1:13 and 2:2; 2 Thess. 2:14 and 3:6; Jude 3; 1 Jn. 2:24 and Heb. 2:1.

Reinforcing all this in more recent times is the mounting archeological and paleographic evidence in Jerusalem attesting to Mary's Assumption.

Using Scripture as a resource, let us consider some of the "indirect" supports of the teaching on Mary's Assumption into heaven. First, consider the "spiritual assumption" that Paul writes about in Ephesians 2:5-6: "God brought us to life with Christ — it is through *grace* that you have been saved — and raised us up with him and gave us a place with him in heaven." For Mary, who was "full of grace" (Lk. 1:28) and whose sacred body enwombed "the Holy One" when the Spirit came upon her and the Most High overshadowed her (vs. 35), it would have been most appropriate for God to preserve that body from death's corruption, as Christ's was (Ps. 16:10; Acts 13:35, 37), and for her to be bodily raised to heaven after the fashion of her divine Son in his Ascension. If grace is divine life in us (see 2 Pet. 1:4) and Mary was "full of grace," then Mary would most appropriately have received that *fullness* of life that Jesus proffers (Jn. 10:10). It was this fullness of divine life which he himself manifested in his own resurrection and ascension, thus prototyping Mary's "ascension" (better referred to as "Assumption," since it did not occur by her own power).

Second, since this "assumption privilege" was extended to Enoch and Elijah — and *possibly* also to those "many holy people" who were resurrected in Jerusalem on that first Good Friday (Mt. 27:52-53), then would it not be even more appropriate for that privilege to be extended to Mary, the one "blessed among all women"?

Third, Mary's immediate "glorification" by being assumed into heaven in a privilege paralleling Jesus' Ascension was most fitting also by reason of the fact that she was so closely conjoined with him in his redemptive suffering on Calvary. Thus, in a preeminent way, Paul's words are applicable to

Mary: "We suffer with him that we may also be glorified with him" (Rom. 8:17).

Fourth, Mary's assumption was a kind of "rapture" that all believers will experience some day as the resurrection of the body (Jn. 5:29; 11:23-24, 1 Cor. 15:52, etc.), although hers was "premature" by comparison. Just as she experienced an *anticipatory* redemption (a sin-preventative redemption rather than a sin-curative one) by the pre-applied merits of her Son at the beginning of her earthly life, so also at the end of her life it was appropriate for her to experience an *anticipatory* "rapture" in being "assumed" bodily into heaven by that same Redeemer, Jesus. It is that same Jesus whom we shall meet in our own "assumption" when we will be "caught up together in the clouds to meet the Lord in the air. . .and be with Him forever" (1 Thess. 4:17). Considering that Mary's Assumption is a privilege that all godly persons will have on the last day, her privilege in this regard doesn't tax our ability to acknowledge it; it is extraordinary only to the extent that it was, unlike ours, prior to the time of the universal "assumption" — that is, the day of the "rapture" or "resurrection of the body," referred to in Scripture and in the Apostles' Creed.

The ancient traditional belief in Mary's bodily Assumption into heaven was declared a dogma by Pope Pius XII in 1950. Like the dogma of the Immaculate Conception, it was not promulgated in reaction to heresy, but in confirmation of a centuries-old belief that had thrived in the Church under the Holy Spirit, who guides the Church "into all truth" (Jn. 16:13). It was not a sudden proclamation resulting from shallow piety, but the culmination of a gradual Scripture-based development of Mariology over many centuries.

Does Scripture help validate the Resurrection of Jesus?

The four Gospels that record the Resurrection story are too similar to be written totally independently of one another, thus

25

affirming one another. Yet they are too dissimilar to one another to be a conspiracy to present a fictional situation as true. Matthew's and John's accounts of the Resurrection clearly show that they were eyewitnesses, not depending on hearsay. Moreover, most of the Gospel writers were willing to accept martyrdom rather than renounce the validity of the Resurrection story. No one will die to defend a lie.

Greater circumstantial evidence is seen in the fact that the cowardly disciples hiding in the upper room later became bold in their proclamation that they had seen Jesus alive; they thus converted three thousand people in one day. They accepted imprisonment and ultimately torturous death rather than deny the truth of the Resurrection, as did thousands of Christians after them.

The risen Christ appeared and talked to more than five hundred people (1 Cor. 15:6), and especially to his disciples on many occasions (Jn. 20: 19-29; 21:1-14; 1 Cor. 15: 5, 7; Lk. 24:15-31, 36, etc). To claim that so many people colluded in a lie or hallucinated is not reasonable.

Why are the seven gifts different from the gifts listed in the New Testament?

The seven gifts of the Holy Spirit differ from the New Testament listings of the charismatic gifts, which do not in themselves sanctify the individual person gifted with them (1 Cor. 13:1-3; Mt. 7:22-23). The so-called "charismatic gifts" are meant to be used altruistically (1 Pet. 4:10), to build up the faith-experience of the community at large (1 Cor. 14: 26); an exception is the charismatic gift of praying in tongues, which as a form of prayer does sanctify the individual, as Paul reminds us (14:4).

Among many Christians today there is an ignorance-based prejudice against charismatic gifts such as tongues, healing, and prophecy — which Paul said all should desire *eagerly* (14:1).

26

Jesus himself affirmed the importance of charismatic gifts among believers, including the gift of tongues (Mk. 16-17), a gift that he himself probably used (Heb. 5:7) in the form of inexpressible utterances that Paul referred to in Rom. 8:26 — the type of heavenly language that *all* 120 persons at the Pentecost event experienced (Acts 2:4), including the Virgin Mary (1:14).

But some abuses of the "charismatic gifts" occurred. Variations of charismatic abuses resulted from the three heresies of Gnosticism, Luminism, and Montanism, thus causing Church authorities to discourage the charismatic gifts, even in confirmation.

This unfortunate discouragement of the charismatic gifts still exists today except in charismatic circles, even though Vatican II encouraged the pursuit of charismatic gifts, (e.g. in the Decree on the Apostolate of the Laity, art. 3), just as Paul himself did (1 Cor. 14:1). Vatican II stated that these charismatic gifts are *instruments of grace*, along with the sacraments, like confirmation.

If Jesus will judge all on the Day of Judgment, why did he tell his Apostles that they would judge the twelve tribes of Israel?

The phrase in the Creed, that Jesus will "come to judge the living and the dead," is supported by many New Testament pericopes (e.g., Mt. 25:32; Jn. 5:22; Acts 10:42; 17-31; Rom. 2:16; 14:10; 2 Tim. 4:1). The task assigned to the twelve Apostles by Jesus to judge the twelve tribes of Israel (Mt. 19:28) is in no way a surrender of Jesus' role as judge. This can be explained in any of three ways:

1) The apostles could exercise this judgment by announcement rather than by pronouncement.

2) Although "all authority in heaven and on earth" was given to Jesus by the Father (Mt. 28:18), he could and did,

during his earthly life, delegate that authority to his Apostles (Mt. 16:19; 18:17-18). His authority as judge on the last day could be delegated in the same way, while maintaining his authority as ultimate Judge of all. Old Testament examples of God's delegation of leadership to Moses and Aaron typify this dynamic (see Psalm 77:20). A parallel example is the Pope's authority, subsidiarized through his apostolic delegates.

3) If the verb "to judge" is interpreted as it is used in the book of Judges, it means "to rule," rather than to judge guilt or innocence. An example was the verb applied to Gideon in Judges 8:23, or the way the Lord was said to "judge" by making decisions or "ruling" on an issue (11:27). In this context the noun would better be translated as "rulers" rather than "judges." The role of judges from Joshua to the time of the monarchy in Israel, is evident from statements like, "The Lord raised up judges who saved them. . . . Yet they would not listen to their judges" (2:16). This implies leadership rather than juridical judgment.

The relationship between the twelve Apostles and the twelve tribes of Israel is found in Revelation 21:12-14. The twelve gates of the heavenly Jerusalem were inscribed with the names of the twelve tribes, while the Apostles were named on the twelve foundations of that Holy City. The symbolic number twelve (implying completeness) for the tribes of God's chosen people finds both replication and continuity in the Apostles as representatives of God's people of the New Testament Church. Probably the "twenty-four elders" (Rev. 4:4, 4:10) are the twelve patriarchs and twelve Apostles that represent both Old and New Testament leaders sitting on the "thrones" from which judgment or subsidiarized leadership could take place.

If the phrase of Jesus "twelve tribes of Israel" is taken as a general symbol signifying all of God's elect of both old and new covenants, then perhaps twelve categories of the elect in heaven will each be under the benign spiritual leadership of one of the twelve Apostles. They in turn will be under the loving guidance of Jesus the Supreme Leader, under whom there is nothing that is not subject (Heb. 2:8).

Is the doctrine of Mary's Immaculate Conception supported in the Bible?

That question might elicit a threefold answer: First, although there are no *direct* references to the doctrine, neither is there anything in Scripture that denies it. (Of course, this negative response *by itself* is not compelling). Second, there are a number of *indirect* scriptural references to support the doctrine, as explained below. And third, there are eight biblical references to support traditions a source of divine revelation — Mary's sinlessness being an *ancient and consistent tradition*, first noted a few years after the death of St. John the Evangelist. (Mary's sinlessness was proclaimed as early as A.D. 370 by St. Ephrem, but implicitly acknowledged as early as 150 A.D.

Such authentic tradition, Vatican II reminds us, is not above Scripture, but "serves" it, helping to interpret it, just as a preacher interprets God's word, "correctly" handling it (2 Tim. 2:15). The Bible tells us to "hold fast to what you have learned," whether by word of mouth or by writing (2 Tim. 3:14).

Other biblical references to tradition as a source of revelation include: 2 Timothy 1:13 and 2:2; 2 Thessalonians 2:14 and 3:6; Jude 3; 1 John 2:24, and Hebrews 2:1.

Let us look at a few of the *indirect* scriptural references to the doctrine of the Immaculate Conception. The Bible affirms that freedom from sin must be God-caused (Ps. 51:10); only by his power could anyone make a claim, "I have been blameless before him and have kept myself from sin" (Ps. 18:23). God speaks of his spotless Bride: "You are all fair, my love; there is no flaw in you" (Song of Songs, 4:7). Mary was uniquely predestined to be the Bride of the Holy Spirit who was to impregnate her (Lk. 1:35). She had to have a sinless body to

29

bear the God Incarnate, Jesus, whom Paul calls "wisdom from God" (1 Cor. 1:30), for "wisdom will not enter a deceitful soul, nor dwell in a body enslaved to sin" (Wis. 1:4).

When did the Bible first include a system of chapter and verse numbering?

Before Gutenberg's invention of movable type, first used in his Bible printed in 1452, hand-copied Bibles were very scarce, and most manuscripts were only sections of the Bible. In those days it was extremely difficult to "look up" anything in the Bible, since the books of the Bible, hand-copied by monks, were not even divided into chapters.

The monumental task of dividing the Bible into chapters and verses was first attempted by Stephen Langton, the Catholic Archbishop of Canterbury, in the late twelfth century, long before printing was invented. He did this with St. Jerome's Latin Vulgate translation of the Bible.

In the following century, Cardinal Hugo undertook to revise Langton's chapter divisions of the Old Testament only. Hugo's chapter divisions were the basis for a later verse division of the Old Testament by Athias, a Jewish scholar from Amsterdam, in 1661.

Meanwhile, the New Testament verse division from Langton was revised by a Dominican friar in the early sixteenth century and re-enumerated by a French painter in 1661 into the verse numbering that we have today in all Christian bibles.

Neither chapter nor verse designation was always made according to the thought of the sacred authors, and the latest versions of the Scriptures are still trying to deal with the awkwardness of many verse divisions, with limited success. Because the early chapter and verse divisions were universally accepted, subsequent attempts at change caused some confusion, especially in parts of the book of Psalms. Since they differed in the Hebrew and Septuagint versions, causing a difference in some parts of the Protestant and Catholic translations, the newer Catholic translations have adapted to the Hebrew bible enumerations used by Protestants. Fortunately, Protestants and Catholics now pretty well agree in their corrections of the older enumerations. This makes for easier dialogue in biblical discussions, article references, Bible research books, etc.

What does the Bible say about guardian angels?

The most direct scriptural reference to such personally assigned angels is found in Jesus' words in Matthew 18, sandwiched between his remarks about childlike humility (perceiving one's own helplessness), and the helplessness of a straying sheep needing rescue. Help for the helpless is provided by personally assigned angels, as Jesus indicates. Though exemplified by a child that Jesus called into his presence, such lowly, weak, and helpless persons (children or adults) are called "little ones," who in God's eyes are not little but great (verse 4).

The greatness or nobility of "the least of his brethren" is highlighted by their being assigned personal angels who are constantly enraptured by the vision of God himself (hence "angel of the Lord" is a common biblical phrase): "See that you do not look down on any one of these little ones. For I tell you that their angels in heaven always see the face of my Father in heaven" (Mt. 18:10). The phrase "any one of these" and the phrase "their angels" indicate that these protectors are not assigned merely as overseers of groups, but even of individuals, that is, as personal guardian angels. That is probably why the early Christians often spoke of an angel as being "his" or "her" angel (see Acts 12:15).

This angelic protection was mentioned even in Old Testament times as not just group protection (Ex. 23:20; Dan. 12:1; 2 Mac. 11:6), but also individualized protection (see Dan.

31

6:22), even though it wasn't until later that rabbinical Jewish angelology taught that there was a personal guardian angel for every individual. David acknowledged some personalism in angelic protection, at least for himself, and hinted it for everyone: "Those who plot my ruin. . .the angel of the Lord drives them away" (Ps. 35:4-5). "This poor man called, and the Lord heard him. . .The angel of the Lord encamps around (each of) those who fear him, and he delivers them" (Ps. 34:6-7). "He will command his angels concerning you to guard you in all your ways" (Ps. 91:11). Even Satan acknowledged this truth about guardian angels, for he quoted that passage when tempting Jesus (Mt. 4:6; Lk. 4:10-11).

Not only guarding but also guiding is seen as a one-to-one function of angels, in cases like that of Abraham's servant (Gen. 24:7), or Hagar's encounter with the angel (Gen. 16:7), or Tobias's guidance by the archangel Raphael (Tobit 5:4).

Besides performing rescue operations (see Dan. 6:22; Acts 5:19; 12:7-11), angels are sent to encourage us in critical situations, as in the case of Paul just before he was shipwrecked (Acts 27:23).

Most of us don't experience angelic apparitions like those mentioned in Scripture; our appreciation of the privilege of having a guardian angel is faith-spawned more often than faith-stimulating. Yet countless people have experienced miraculous protection from their guardian angels, and many have even been helped by persons suspected of being angels in human disguise —a possibility mentioned in Hebrews 13:2.

Wasn't St. Paul unfairly opposed to women's liberation?

Paul, who is often unfairly regarded as anti-feminist, did refuse to allow women to teach men or to dominate them, using Adam's priority and Eve's deception as the rationale (1 Tim. 2:12-14); but this was his scriptural support for adaptation to the local culture that asserted male superiority at Ephesus, and a way of coping with the deception of untrained and aggressive Ephesian women engaged in false teaching there. Under different circumstances this prohibition was not meant to apply — as when Priscilla taught Apollos (Acts 18:26). Also, Paul did forbid women to speak in church (1 Cor. 14:35) in a disorderly manner (chattering during the services), although he did not forbid them to speak out in church in prayer or prophecy (11:5). Paul did seem to speak only of male elders (priests) in 1 Tim. 3:1-7; yet, like Jesus, he welcomed women as co-workers in his ministry (Phil. 4:3). Male and female, he said, are "one in Christ Jesus" (Gal. 3:28), and elsewhere he staunchly professed women's equality with men in God's eyes (1 Cor. 11:11-12).

Doesn't the Bible see women as second-class citizens?

It is true that women, especially in Old Testament times, were regarded as second-class citizens in many legal situations. The first example in Scripture of women pleading for their rights before the judges and leaders of a nation was when the five daughters of Zelophehad demanded inheritance rights, and God himself stood up for them in their demands. "When Moses brought their case before the Lord, the Lord said to him, 'What Zelophehad's daughters are saying is right. You must certainly give them property as an inheritance' " (Num. 27:5-7). Moses was told by God of women's basic equality with men in his eyes, by granting them the same privilege of consecration to him by the Nazirite vow (6:2). Furthermore, God chose women to accomplish many of his special purposes (e.g. Ruth, Rahab, Esther, Deborah, Sarah, etc.).

Later the Jewish Pharisaic revolution upgraded women's status and enacted numerous laws to protect them, although it did not permit women in the houses of study or allow them to become rabbis. (Mysogynism dies a slow death, usually, with only token rights granted at first.)

When Jesus came onto the scene he boldly initiated a "Christian feminist movement." At Jacob's well at Sychar, he contravened anti-feminist customs and shocked his disciples, who "were surprised to find him talking with a woman" (Jn. 4:27), since Jewish religious leaders rarely spoke with women in public. He then shocked the Pharisees by pointing out the superiority of a repentant woman sinner over a man who looked on her with disdain (Lk. 7:36-47). He accepted women in his ministry and entourage, who were with him in his travels from Galilee to Calvary (Lk. 23:55). These included converted street women, like Mary Magdalene, as well as noble women like Joanna, wife of Herod's household manager; Susanna, and "many other women" (Lk. 8:2-3). It was to women, not men, that Jesus first appeared after the resurrection (Mt. 28:9).

Early Christianity continued to build on Christ's recognition of women's rights and dignity, especially after the Virgin Mary attained preeminence and esteem, and was associated with other women at the Pentecost experience (Acts 1:14).

Doesn't Jesus say that John the Baptist is a reincarnation of the prophet Elijah?

There are those who make a claim for reincarnation by citing Jesus' claim, in Matthew 11:14, that John the Baptist "is the Elijah who was to come." This is one of five passages in the gospels mentioning John as the predicted appearance of "Elijah" in the prophecy of Malachi.

Malachi prophesies twice about a future precursor: "I will send my messenger, who will prepare the way before me" (3:1; Jesus quotes this in Mt. 11:10). Malachi's other prophecy is in the next chapter (4:5-6): "I will send you the prophet Elijah before that great and dreadful day of the Lord comes. He will turn the hearts of the fathers to their children, and the hearts of the children to their fathers." This double prophecy spelled out the same double mission assigned to John the Baptist, to be carried out "in the spirit and power of Elijah," as the angel Gabriel told John's father, Zechariah (Lk. 1:17).

John was not Elijah returning in the flesh, for he clearly stated that he was not Elijah, and again that he was not the prophet (John 1:21), but he functioned like that Old Testament preacher of repentance, and was therefore a fulfillment of Malachi's double prophecy about an Elijah figure. Jesus referred to this in Matthew 11:14 and 17:10-13 (see also Mk. 9:11-13).

Jesus said that John was a prophet and more than a prophet (Mt. 11:9; Lk. 7:26). Why did John staunchly claim that he was not the prophet (John 1:21)? The Jews remembered that Elijah, the greatest Old Testament prophet, had not died, but was transported to heaven in a fiery chariot (2 Kings 2:11); and, following Malachi's prophecy, they believed that he would return (still alive) to announce the "end time."

In this sense John properly denied that he was the prophet Elijah; John knew he was called to be the forerunner of Christ at the first coming, while Elijah was to be Christ's forerunner at the second coming, "that great and dreadful day of the Lord," as Malachi prophesied. This parallelism, among others, led Jesus to refer to John as an "Elijah," but not to establish that John was Elijah reincarnated.

Even if the reincarnationists were correct in saying that John was actually Elijah in the flesh, it still would not prove their theory. There would have been no soul transmigration because, not having died, Elijah's soul never left his body. The person called John would then have been Elijah in his own body, not that of another, and hence no reincarnation. Of course this scenario didn't occur, but if it had, it would not authenticate reincarnation as a doctrine. John, of course received his body from his parents, Zechariah and Elizabeth (Lk. 1:13).

Moreover, John became Spirit-filled in his mother's womb (Lk. 1:41). Elijah was also Spirit-filled, even to being miraculously transported by the Spirit (1 Kings 18:12; 2 Kings 2:16). These were obviously two separate actions of the Spirit, filling two distinctly separate souls in two separate bodies at two separate times. It was not one Spirit-filled soul needing a refilling after its transmigration.

After his rapture (2 Kings 2:12), Elijah's power, not personhood or identity, was transferred to Elisha. Likewise, a power (like the charism of conversion-preaching), but not personhood or identity, could have been transferred much later to John the Baptist, making him another "Elijah." God could assign Elijah's power, but not his soul, to John.

The angel's prophecy to Zechariah (Lk. 1:17) said that John's power would be that of Elijah, not his soul or personhood, as would be the case in reincarnation. Their similarity was also in holiness (Mt. 11:11), and repentance-preaching (Mk. 1:4; Lk. 16:1).

Finally, if Elijah had been reincarnated as John the Baptist, he would have appeared in the person of John at the transfiguration scene, but he appeared as himself — Elijah, conversing with Jesus (see Mt. 17:3; Mk. 9:4; Lk. 9:30).

What does the Bible say about reincarnation?

Anyone believing either the Old or New Testament would be forced to reject reincarnation. Samuel's posthumous communication with Saul showed that Samuel retained his identity after death (1 Sam. 28:14). Isaiah 14:9 says, "The grave below is all astir to meet you at your coming; it rouses the spirits of the departed to greet you." Disembodied "spirits of the departed" are not reincarnated spirits; otherwise they would be living persons. "If a tree is cut down it will sprout again . . . but man dies. . .breathes his last and is no more" (Job 14:7-10). "He will never see the light of life again" (Ps. 49:19). All Old Testament references to post-death experiences exclude any possibility of reincarnation.

In the New Testament, likewise, reincarnation is clearly out of the question. Paul's yearning for heaven led him to "prefer to be away from the body and at home with the Lord" (2 Cor. 5:8). He doesn't yearn for or expect to be away from the body by entering another body. Again Paul affirms this in his letter to the Philippians: "If I am to go on living in my body, it will mean fruitful labor for me. . . . Yet I desire to depart and to be with Christ" (Phil. 1:22-23). He was consoled by Jesus' dictum that those in heaven "can no longer die" (Lk. 20:36).

St. John in his vision (Rev. 6:9) saw the slain souls under the altar, not reincarnated in other bodies as other persons. Jesus' parable of the rich man and Lazarus (Lk. 16:19-31) speaks of the former going to Hades immediately after his death, and the latter to Abraham's side; neither was described by Jesus as having been reincarnated after death.

New Agers claim that reincarnation teachings were deliberately deleted from the Bible by the Church Councils; yet they quote the Bible to "prove" reincarnation — in passages like Jesus' reference to Elijah. Obviously, if the Church Councils did attempt to delete reincarnation references, why would they have left any references to it in the Bible? The Jews jealously preserved intact their Hebrew Bible, and yet it is the same as the Christian Old Testament; also, the Dead Sea scrolls confirm the Bible's ageless nonvariance, thus debunking the deletion theory.

If New Testament passages or books had been deleted, that would have required collecting all extant New Testaments throughout the literate world and redistributing new renditions in their place — clearly an absurd conjecture. The Gnostic books proclaiming reincarnation, along with the heresy that Jesus was a mere "Levantine magician," had never been accepted as part of the Bible, as claimed by reincarnationists, because of such blatant Christological heresies.

In summary, no Bible-believer could ever accept the false doctrine of reincarnation. Any scriptural references appearing to validate it — such as references to John the Baptist as Elijah

— on close examination, are seen as totally unsupportive of such a perverted doctrine.

An interesting postscript to this is the observation of many spiritual directors, that an extraordinarily high percentage of Christians who continue to hold to the pseudo-doctrine of reincarnation eventually drift away from regular church attendance and reception of the sacraments. Later they often become infected with a spirit of occultism. In the "end times" such false doctrines will lead many astray, warns Paul — persons who "are always learning but never able to acknowledge the truth" (2 Tim. 3:7). "The Spirit says that in later times some will abandon the faith and follow deceiving spirits" (1 Tim. 4:1).

His timely advice (Col. 2:8) is worth reflecting on: "See to it that no one takes you captive through hollow and deceptive philosophy, which depends on human tradition and the basic principles of this world rather than on Christ."

How did the Church decide what should be included in the Catholic Bible?

The criteria for determining New Testament canonicity — that is, for knowing which Christian books were inspired and hence worthy of being included in the New Testament — are drawn indirectly from remarks by the early Fathers of the Church. These criteria include: 1) origin in apostolic times; 2) the reception and continued use of the documents by the early congregations of Christians; 3) the consistency of doctrine with all that had been accepted before the documents appeared; 4) a common appreciation of the books which time and use confirmed in preaching and public prayer. The criteria for Old Testament canonicity were somewhat similar, except for apostolic timing.

It is obvious that the formation and acceptance of both Old and New Testament canons among Christians was ultimately an act of intuition of the Church, under Jesus' promised guidance of the Holy Spirit (Jn. 14:26).

Two underlying elements were obviously present in the formation of both Old and New Testament canons: 1) tradition, and 2) the magisterium of the Church in councils that defined the specific list of inspired works. Both of these elements are repudiated by Protestantism as sources of revealed truth, yet it finds itself compelled to accept both of them in embracing the New Testament canon. At Luther's instigation, Protestantism rejected the principle of tradition, yet accepted Jewish tradition as a basis for the Hebrew canon it finally embraced. It rejected the Catholic magisterium as determining the Old Testament canon, but it seemed to accept a kind of "magisterium" of the Jews in their "Council of Jamnia" about A.D. 90 and/or the "men of the Great Synagogue" referred to in the Talmud that presumably determined the Hebrew canon.

Some Protestants do not accept all of the Catholic Bible, namely the seven and a half books that Luther excluded when he adopted the Hebrew (Palestinian) canon rather than the Alexandrian canon. However, up until quite recently almost all Protestant Bibles, like the King James version from 1611, contained these deuterocanonical books in a kind of appendix which was titled "Apocrypha."

Notwithstanding the canonicity controversy concerning the Old Testament, there is common agreement between Catholics and Protestants on the vast majority of the Bible. And among Protestant scholars there is a great respect for the content, beauty and historicity of the deuterocanonical books, which they regard as non-inspired but inspiring. This augurs well for the success of ecumenical endeavors that depend so much on concurrence in biblical matters, as well as for successful collaboration on scriptural research projects.

Why are some books in Catholic translations of the Bible but not in some Protestant versions?

Determining which books belong in the Bible was a process that took centuries. The list or "canon" of the Old Testament (Hebrew Bible) was not established even by the Jews themselves until after the time of Jesus. And the early Christian Church was still debating some New Testament writings well into the fourth century, even though the twenty-seven books of the New Testament had been written roughly between A.D. 55 and 100.

Protestants did not *always* agree with the Catholic canon of the New Testament that had been established at the Council of Hippo in 393 and the Third Council of Carthage in 397. In the sixteenth century, Martin Luther regarded four books — Hebrews, James, Jude, and Revelation — as inferior and put them at the end of his New Testament translation in a detached position. Calvin seems to have had reservations about 2 and 3 John, and this policy was followed by the Lutheran church until the seventeenth century. (Even though these books were published as a kind of appendix of the bible, Lutherans of those days did not regard them as inspired by God.) Eventually, all of Protestantism came to accept the complete Catholic canon for the New Testament as defined by the Council of Trent in 1546, which reconfirmed the New Testament canon that had been compiled in the two Catholic councils in the fourth century.

The Old Testament canon is another matter. Martin Luther rejected the Catholic Church's traditional canon taken from the Septuagint (Greek) version used by the Hellenistic Jews in Alexandria, and chose rather the Hebrew canon used by the Jews in Palestine. By doing this, Luther dropped seven and a half books from the Old Testament that had been accepted by all Christians prior to that time — namely, Tobit, Judith, Wisdom, Sirach (Ecclesiasticus), Baruch, 1 and 2 Maccabees, and part of Daniel called the book of Susanna. These seven and a half books were classified by Protestants among the many "Apocrypha" (non-inspired religious books). Catholics refer to them as "deuterocanonical" (second canon) books, while referring to "apocryphal" works as any non-canonical religious treatises.

The Septuagint version of the Old Testament in which these books are found is the version from which are taken most of the Old Testament quotations found in the New Testament, including those quoted by Jesus. Also all of the Septuagint books are found in the recently discovered Dead Sea scrolls, with the exception of Esther.

The deuterocanonical books contained in the Septuagint fill in some of the intertestamental gap of 400 years between the end of the Hebrew Bible and the New Testament times. But the canonicity of the seven and a half books was questioned in the fourth century A.D., which explains why St. Jerome placed them in a special section of his Latin Vulgate translation of the Old Testament. But after the Council of Trent declared them canonical, there was no longer any question among Catholics about their canonicity.

How does the Church see the text in Revelation which says that good people will "reign with Christ for a thousand years"?

This prophetic reference is found in Revelation 20. The "thousand years" is referred to as the "Millennium" (from the Latin mille, "thousand" and annus, "year"). It is often taken literally as one thousand actual years, while others interpret it metaphorically or symbolically as a long but undetermined period of time. There are three basic approaches to this matter of the so-called millennium:

1) Amillennialism. This opinion holds that the millennium describes the present reign of the souls in heaven with Christ, and that this present form of God's kingdom will be followed by the second coming of Christ, the general resurrection of the dead, with the final judgment and Christ's continuing reign

over the perfect heavenly kingdom lasting a "thousand years" — symbolizing eternity.

This opinion cannot be easily reconciled with Revelation 20:5, where there is a mention of the "thousand years" ending. But another amillennialist position regards the "thousand years" as symbolic of the period between the first and second comings of Christ. (For this period, Satan may be said to be "bound" (vs. 2) — that is, restricted by the power of Christ's redemptive act of Calvary.) St. Augustine held that the "thousand years" is the Christian era from the time of Christ's Resurrection until his second coming — the period presently in progress. Any of these variations of amillennialism may be held by Catholics, doctrinally.

2) Premillennialism. This second category of interpretation claims that when Christ returns he will establish a visible, literal government on earth in space-time history; this will merge into the eternal kingdom after a thousand years, when the resurrection and last judgment will take place. Then he will reign forever on the new earth. This literal millenarianism was condemned by the Catholic Church in a Decree of the Holy Office, July 19, 1944, by Pope Pius XII, although it had been a widespread opinion in the early Church. The Church's teaching associates Christ's second coming (*Parousia*) proximately with the resurrection of the dead ("rapture"), with final judgment, and with the glory of his eternal kingdom (as indicated in Jn. 5:29; 14:3-4; 1 Thess. 4:16-17; 5:10; Col. 3:4, etc.).

3) Postmillennialism. This third opinion (which is doctrinally acceptable for Catholics) holds that the world will eventually be Christianized, resulting in a long period (symbolically, a thousand years of peace and prosperity called the millennium), which will close with Christ's second coming, the resurrection of the dead ("rapture"), the final judgment and then eternity. This position fits well with the numerous passages, especially in the Old Testament, regarding future earthly peace and prosperity prior to the end of the world.

Literal millenarianism (sometimes called "chiliasm")

started with Jewish converts to Christianity in Asia Minor. Many modern fundamentalists and other religious groups adhere to this literal notion of one thousand years of Christ's future reign on earth after the final judgment.

The general Catholic position is that the millennium means an age of grace wherein the faithful are living, whether on earth or in heaven. The Church does not encourage naïve literalism in the interpretation of symbolic expressions used in Scripture to describe the end of history; it can lead to misreadings of God's revelation when the literary genre is apocalyptic.

What is the charismatic gift of prophecy as it is described in the New Testament?

Prophecy — the greatest of the twenty-five charismatic gifts mentioned in the New Testament — is a gift by which God speaks through a personal message to an individual, or more commonly to a community. It is usually a "*vaticinium*" form of prophecy, which is not futuristic or predictive but a means by which God speaks to his people "for their strengthening, encouragement, and comfort," as Paul says (1 Cor. 14:3). It is be sought eagerly by all (vs. 1), but it is to be used "in a fitting and orderly way" (vs. 40), with appropriate self-control (vss. 29-33). When this great gift is used properly, in accordance with Paul's norms, it truly does draw the hearers to the Lord and deepens their sense of his presence which leaves them with the triple effect as Paul states: strengthened, encouraged, and comforted. Vatican II reminds us that such charisms are "fitting and useful for the needs of the Church" (*Lumen Gentium*, art. 12). Even on those rare occasions when the prophecy is directed to an individual, it still must be ultimately for the common good (1 Cor. 12:7; 1 Pet. 4:10; Eph. 4:16; see art. 3 of *Apostolicam Actuositatem*, the Vatican II document on the laity).

A true prophecy encourages, builds up, consoles, or

reaffirms God's love. Occasionally it may come as a gentle reprimand that leads to repentance. It is never condemnatory, even when sorrow-filled, as was Jesus' prophecy over Jerusalem (Mt. 23:37), with more love than judgment in its tone.

A false prophecy from the evil one is quite rare and easily recognized as angry, hate-filled, or disruptive in its timing, or unscriptural in its content. It strikes fear or coldness in the hearts of the listeners, definitely never extols Jesus as Lord and Savior (Rev. 19:10), and doesn't inspire one to praise God.

Far more common is non-prophecy from the human spirit, motivated by a desire to air a pet peeve, or a prideful desire to be in the spotlight. In general, this type of prophecy just doesn't ring true to most listeners and "clutters" the prayer meeting, retarding the flow of the Holy Spirit. Yet any sincere person who has only a weak anointing, like most beginners in the renewal, may have an unwarranted fear of thus "cluttering" the meeting with non-prophecy. If in doubt, one should speak out the prophecy after silent prayer, and wait for the community to discern the utterance (1 Cor. 14:29; 1 Thess. 5:21). Thus used with humility the weak gift will grow in time (Phil. 3:12-14).

With so many people today attracted to spiritism, the occult, psychic revelations, "channeling," etc., it is good to know that God offers us a gift from his Holy Spirit that far transcends in beauty these perverted forms of seeking arcane knowledge. And it is assuring to know that his holy Word and Spirit-guided Church provide norms of authenticity to protect us from dangers that could arise from desiring something beyond what our senses could provide. "We have not received the spirit of the world but the Spirit who is from God, that we may understand what God has freely given us. This is what we speak, not in words taught us by human wisdom, but in words taught by the Spirit, expressing spiritual truths in spiritual words" (1 Cor. 2:12-13).

What does the Bible say about gambling?

Money, of course, is not evil, but "the love of money is the root of all kinds of evil. Some people, eager for money, have wandered from the faith and pierced themselves with many griefs" (1 Tim. 6:10). Gambling seems to carry its own momentum; it is not too hard to overspend what is reasonable; borderline compulsive gamblers can easily go over the line into full addiction, which is extremely difficult to correct. Perhaps that's what Paul had in mind when he wrote, "people who want to get rich fall into temptation and a trap, and into many foolish and harmful desires that plunge men into ruin and destruction" (1 Tim. 6:9).

Gambling-related evils mentioned in Scripture include materialism, greed, sloth, avarice, profligacy, imprudence, and recklessness. Serious gamblers should study the texts: those poisoned with materialism should heed the words of Psalm 62:10: "Though your riches increase, do not set your heart on them" (see also Job 31:24-25; Mt. 19:23). Greed-motivated gambling would also indirectly contravene Scripture (Lk. 12:15; Heb. 13:5; Phil. 4:10-13; 1 Tim. 6:17-19; 3:3, etc.). Gambling as a substitute for honest labor is also proscribed by Scripture (Prov. 12:11,28:19). "A faithful person will be richly blessed (with God's gifts and favors), but one eager to get rich will not go unpunished" (Prov. 20:21, 23:4, 15:27, etc.). Many a gambler has, like the prodigal son, "squandered his wealth in wild living" (Lk. 15:13). Any gambling that involves reckless investment of God-given resources (as in imprudent stock market speculation, rather than cautious investment) would parallel the situation of the "worthless servant" who buried his master's money (Mt. 25:27).

On the other side of coin (excuse the flippant pun), the Bible does not explicitly condemn gambling. Matthias was chosen to replace Judas by the casting of lots, after prayer (Acts 1:26). Prayerfully allowing God the right of choice by lots is a chance-based activity analogous to gambling. Proverbs 16:33 says, "The lot is cast, but its every decision is from the Lord" — implying that God, not chance, is in control ultimately (see

45

verses 1, 3, 4, and 9). "Chance," the presumed basis of gambling, is a misnomer for Divine Providence, said St. Thomas Aquinas. Urim and Thummim (sacred lots) were used in Old Testament times to determine the will of God (Ex. 28:30; Num. 27:21; 26:56; Neh. 11:1; Jon. 1:7; 1 Chron. 26:13; 1 Sam. 14:41, etc.,) but only in matters of major consequence. Casting lots was used by pagans also, when consulting idols (Ezek. 21:21) — a custom used today in Taoism and other religions. To see how easily the use of prayerful, God-directed acts of "chance" can thus be perverted, witness the frequent use of the quasi-pagan term "Lady Luck" in gambling situations. Very few gamblers prayerfully seek God's will in their games of chance; most seek only money.

Why does the Church teach that Jesus was an only child when Scripture says that He had brothers and sisters?

This often-asked question, insistently asked since the fourth century, is mainly based on Matthew 13:55-56 and 12:46, which speak of Jesus' "brothers and sisters," pointing up a conflict with the Church's tradition of Mary being "ever virgin." Mary's "first-born" (Lk. 2:7) was of course Jesus; that term was applied to the firstborn, whether other children followed or not, according to Jewish idiom (Ex. 13:2). The words "brother and sister" (often translated "brethren") can mean, as the Greek dictionary says, "near or remote" brethren or relatives. In both Hebrew and western Aramaic (the language used by Jesus and those around him in Palestine at that time), there was no specific word for cousin, uncle, aunt, so near kinsfolk were referred to as "brothers and sisters," especially in the extended or patriarchal family of the time. Like the Hebrew word for brother (*ach*), so also the Greek word (*adelphos*) was given the same extended meaning of kinsman, not necessarily a sibling relative, in New Testament (*Koine*) Greek. This led to the ambiguity about whether Jesus had sibling brothers and sisters (see also Jn. 2:12 and Acts 1:14).

There are many Old Testament examples of the same confusion: Lot was Abram's brother's son (Gen. 12:5), yet Abram called him "brother" (13:8); Tobias called his second cousin Sara his "sister" several times (Tobit, 8:4 and 7), etc.

Jesus' four "brothers" are mentioned by name in Matthew 13:55: James, Joseph (Joses), Simon and Judas (Jude). Certainly James and Joseph (Joses) were not sons of Mary, the mother of Jesus, since they are listed as sons of another Mary at the foot of the cross in Matthew 27:56 and Mark 15:40 — the "other Mary" mentioned in Matthew 27:61. Yet they are listed as "brothers" of Jesus — an example of the semantic confusion that could lead to the conclusion that Christ had siblings — contrary to the consistent tradition from the early Church which held these "brothers and sisters" to be Jesus' "brethren." Otherwise, why would Jesus consign the care of Mary at the foot of the cross to John "the disciple" (Jn. 19:26), who was not Jesus' brother. And John's own disciple, St. Polycarp, writes that Mary was perpetually a virgin.

Could Mary have had stepchildren from Joseph by a former marriage of his? This is possible but not probable, since a pious and ancient tradition holds that Joseph never lost his virginity — a tradition almost as strong as that of Mary's perpetual virginity. Ancient artists portrayed Joseph with a lily as a symbol of his perpetual celibacy. The Church follows Paul's command to "hold fast to those traditions passed on to you by word of mouth or by letter" (2 Thess. 2:15). The ancient Nicene Creed thus calls Mary "ever virgin." Biblical linguistics support this Catholic position regarding Jesus as an only child of Mary, not just the "only begotten Son of the Father."

Catholic Leadership and Authority

If we already have the Holy Spirit dwelling within us, why do we need the clergy or the Pope to help us interpret Scripture?

Let us consider the assertion that no mediumship or mediation is needed to interpret God's word. For most of Scripture, that is true. That's another way of saying that the Church permits freedom of interpretation of Scripture for most of the biblical passages. In fact, the Catholic Church probably grants more freedom of interpretation than most Protestant denominations do, for they have very strictly defined explanations of critical passages, not allowing for much leeway for the private judgment of their members on such issues as water baptism, infant baptism, divorce and remarriage, faith related to works, the doctrine of the Eucharist, Peter's primacy, the role of tradition in revelation, etc.

Protestantism began with Luther advocating private interpretation of Scripture, reasoning that if the Pope could interpret the Bible, why couldn't anyone else? But his sermons and writings later in life indicated that he retreated from that position after seeing the disastrous results of having unqualified persons equating their knowledge to that of Scripture scholars.

" 'Do you understand what you are reading?' Philip asked the eunuch. 'How can I,' he said 'unless someone explains it to me?' " (Acts 8:30-31). God expects us to make use of human guidance in spiritual matters as well as in non-spiritual education. Otherwise all seminaries, Bible schools and Sunday school classes would be obliged to shut down.

Peter wrote that Paul's epistles "contain some things that are hard to understand, which ignorant and unstable people distort, as they do the other Scriptures, to their own destruction ... be on your guard that you may not be carried away by the error. . ." (2 Pet. 3:16-17).

Clearly, the Bible points up the need for religious leaders as "overseers" (1 Pet. 5:2), preachers (4:11), teachers (Rom. 12:7), leaders (vs.8), and also the obligation to respect and obey them (1 Thess. 5:12; 1 Tim. 5:17; Heb. 13:17). Even a casual reading of Scripture will show that God designed that the Kingdom should be built by guidance and instruction of God, directed through human instruments (Mt. 28:19-20; Rom. 12:16). To arrogantly ignore those divinely appointed instruments is to defy the design of God himself, and truth sought in that manner will have only "the appearance of wisdom" with "self-imposed worship" and "false humility" (Col. 2:23).

Countless examples in the New Testament attest to the fact that preaching, administration of sacraments, and also interpretation of Scripture itself are performed by a sacred minister between an individual believer and Christ. Of course these acts of mediation are in no way obstacles to union with God, but are facilitators of that union.

A Catholic who truly understands the Church's role in scriptural interpretation is very uninhibited in reading the Bible. Catholics are instructed to read a given passage according to the intent of the sacred author, which is usually clear from the context of the passage itself or of the entire book. If that fails to yield a clear understanding, the Catholic consults the accumulated wisdom of the Church.

The Vatican II document on Divine Revelation (*Dei Verbum*) puts it this way: "The task of authentically interpreting the word of God, whether written or handed on, has been entrusted exclusively to the living teaching office of the Church, whose authority is exercised in the name of Jesus Christ. This teaching office is not above the word of God, but serves it, teaching only what has been handed on, listening to it devoutly, guarding it scrupulously, and explaining it faithfully by divine commission and with the help of the Holy Spirit; it draws from this one deposit of faith everything which it presents for belief as divinely revealed" (no. 10).

As Father Raymond Brown points out in the *Jerome Biblical Commentary*, the Church exercises great restraint in offering authoritative interpretations of individual verses; fewer than a dozen such instances can be pointed to in her two-thousand-year history, most of them at the Council of Trent, and never in matters such as authorship or dating of a book. Hence the Church certainly doesn't use a heavy hand to stifle private interpretation, but presents official interpretations of such things as Petrine (papal) primacy in Matthew 16:17-19 and John 21:15-19, or James 5:14 as related to the sacrament of the anointing of the sick, and the literal interpretation of the accounts in John 6, attesting to the Real Presence of Christ in the Eucharist.

To insist on one's own interpretation on points contrary to twenty centuries of authentic, authoritative, and scholarly understanding of a particular passage would be an inexcusable form of sheer arrogance.

Catholic Piety and Practice

What is the "Easter duty"?

The so-called "Easter duty" is often misunderstood. It remains as it always has, since the Fourth Lateran Council in 1215. Church law (canon 920) states that all Catholics who have received their First Holy Communion are obliged to receive Communion (non-sacrilegiously, of course) at least once a year, and that this must be done during the Easter season, which in the United States has been extended from the first Sunday of Lent to Trinity Sunday — a period of about 14 weeks. If one has a very good reason for not doing so (such as living in an extremely remote priestless area, or being confined in an institution where the sacraments are not available) the obligation may be fulfilled at another time, if and when possible.

Contrary to popular belief, there is no obligation to confess one's sins during the Easter season, but there is an obligation to confess serious sins at least once a year (canon 989); that is, one must not wait longer than a year after committing a *serious* sin to confess it to a priest; and of course, during that period the person must refrain from receiving Communion (even if that sin has meanwhile been forgiven by an act of perfect contrition).

If no confessor is physically or "morally" available when there's a grave reason for receiving Communion (such as the need to preserve one's reputation that would be damaged by abstaining from Communion), then the person who had *seriously* sinned may receive Communion after making an act of perfect contrition (i.e., one based on love of God, not just dread of divine punishment). But in this exceptional case, the person must have the intention of confessing as soon as reasonably possible (canon 916).

**Why is Sunday celebrated as the "Sabbath" when
Scripture says that the Creator "rested" on the seventh day,
after His six days of creation?**

During Passover week in ancient times, with the feast of
the Unleavened Bread, Sunday — the day after the Sabbath —
was regarded as sacred, a day of work-free rest and sacred
assembly (Lev. 23:6-7), with its liturgical act of waving of the
first fruit sheaf by the priest and the sacrifice of the yearling
lamb (verses 11-12). Likewise, the Jewish feast of Weeks
(Pentecost) seven weeks later, always fell on Sunday, the first
day of the week, and was sanctified by refraining from work
and by a sacred assembly (vss. 20-21). So in Old Testament
times, at least several times a year, Sunday as well as Saturday
was to be kept holy. Thus at least a partial precedent to later
changes in the Christian era was found in the Old Testament, in
the prototyped feasts that presaged the Christian feasts of
Easter and Pentecost.

The Christian custom of assigning Sunday instead of
Saturday as a day of religious celebration, was possibly started
by Paul or at least recognized by him (1 Cor. 16:2) as a time for
a monetary collection for the needy in Jerusalem. These
first-day-of-the-week collections undoubtedly took place at the
weekly assembly, not house by house. Since the celebration of
the Lord's Supper had been commanded by Jesus as a repeated
service (Lk. 22:19), it was observed regularly (Acts 2:42); and
we know this occurred on Sunday because Paul preached at
these assemblies that focused on the "Breaking of the Bread"
(Lord's Supper or Eucharist), as Scripture says, on the first day
of the week, Sunday (Acts 20:7).

The early Christians referred to this day of religious
celebration as the "Lord's Day," as Theodoret reminds us. This
was a term that gained apostolic and scriptural sanction by
being referred to by John in Revelation 1:10. (If he had meant
Saturday, he would have used the word "Sabbath").

It was called the "Lord's Day," says St. John Chrysostom

in his sermon on Psalm 119, because it was the day that the Lord rose from the dead, "the first day of the week" according to all four Gospels. As Christianity's cornerstone event (1 Cor. 15:17), Jesus' resurrection symbolized the new life with which he endowed his mystical Body; as such, it was regarded as an appropriate day of the week to manifest that newly endowed corporate life, by corporately praising God and being renewed in that resurrection life with the life-nourishing Eucharist.

Not just the new life of Jesus' physical Body (on Easter), but also the beginning of the life of his mystical Body, the Church (Pentecost) took place on Sunday — both appropriately on the first day of the week to symbolize the new covenant that Jesus established a "new birth into a living hope" (1 Pet. 1:3) — a rationale for the Lord's Day asserted by several early Fathers of the Church. Thus, at the start of the week, the Christians celebrated their two major starting points: that of their new personal life in Christ (the Resurrection), and that of their new communitarian life in Christ (Pentecost). These corresponded exactly to the two Jewish Sunday Feasts mentioned in Leviticus 23:7 and 16.

The early Christians, being Jews by nationality, simply added to Judaism the beliefs and practice of Christianity, since Jesus "came not to abolish, but to fulfill" (Mt. 5:17). Thus, though they prayed in the temple, they also celebrated the Eucharist in their homes (Acts 2:46). Their "liturgy of the word," in the temple was on the Sabbath, Saturday, but their "liturgy of the Eucharist" — the Christian addition to their worship — was celebrated on Sunday (Acts 20:7), so as not to conflict with the Jewish practices in which they participated. This was the origin of the practice of Sunday worship by Christians.

The orthodox Jews eventually excommunicated the Christians from Judaism and expelled them from the temple and synagogues (Acts 8:1). At this point the Christians retrenched the double liturgy from a Saturday-Sunday celebration into one service on Sunday — a double liturgy which exists today in the two continuous parts of the Mass — the liturgy of the word and the liturgy of the Eucharist.

The Jewish obligation of the Sabbath law requiring religious observance and abstinence from work was incorporated into Catholic Church law but applied to Sundays. Obligatory Mass attendance by Catholics has been mitigated in modern times to allow the fulfillment of this obligation on Saturday afternoon in many places, thus "overlapping" the Catholic law with the Jewish Sabbath law, and allowing Catholics the option of a more literal way to "keep holy the Sabbath." This also allows more time for Sunday relaxation and prayer time. Sunday must still be "kept holy" by avoiding unnecessary work and shopping.

One may wonder by what authority the Church can alter God's commandment about the Sabbath, by either changing the day, or imposing Mass obligation, etc. — a question often asked by Seventh Day Adventists and similar groups. Keep in mind that there is no essential feature of the law that has been changed, but that secondary part which has been modified (being not intrinsic to divine law) was determined by power granted by Jesus himself to the Church to "bind or loose" on earth with a recognition of any such decision in heaven (Mt. 16:19, 18:18). The Church has always used this power to make ecclesiastical (canon) laws with sanctions (under penalty of sin). Obedience to these laws, derived from ecclesiastical authority, is demanded by God's word itself (1 Thess. 5:12; Heb. 13:17; Acts 20:28, etc.).

Most Protestant denominations reject Catholic traditions based on papal or hierarchical authority. But in this matter (as in the acceptance of all and only the twenty-seven books of the New Testament canon) they have, for the most part, accepted the ancient Catholic tradition, even though it is perhaps something of a theological embarrassment to them to do so. But the near unanimity on this matter among Christians reaffirms the fact that it is scripturally acceptable and not contrary to God's will.

Why do we Catholics refer to our priests as "Father" when Jesus said that our only Father was the One in heaven?

In Matthew 23:9, Jesus says to call no man father, or teacher, or rabbi. Those of fundamentalist persuasions take this quite literally, but tend to downplay the reference to teacher and rabbi in everyday practice. The context of Jesus' statement was to prohibit the seeking of prideful titles that could possibly derogate the supreme authority of God; taken out of this context, parents could not allow their children to refer to their male parent by such an address.

Paul puts the issue in context by assuming the role of "spiritual father": "You are my children" (2 Cor. 12:14, Living Bible). He claimed a spiritual fatherhood as a "life-conveyor" by his conveying the life of the Gospel message to his "children": "I am writing to warn and counsel you as beloved children . . . remember that you have only me as your father, for I was the one who brought you to Christ when I preached the Gospel to you" (1 Cor. 4:14-15 LB). "I speak as to my children" (2 Cor. 6:13). And to the Thessalonians: "We dealt with each of you as a father deals with his own children" (1 Thess. 2:11).

In the first and third epistles of John we see the phrase "dear children" or "my dear children" used repeatedly as he assumes the position of spiritual fatherhood in guiding those whom he has lead to a new birth in the Lord. Paul refers to Timothy as being "like a son" to him (1 Tim. 1:2 LB).

A spiritual fatherhood or parenthood is not something outside of God's plan for spiritual leaders, for he has promised spiritual children (Is. 54:1-3) and foster fathers to his chosen ones (Is.49:23). For this reason the title "Father" has been used in recent centuries to address the clergy of Orthodox, Anglican, Episcopalian, and Catholic churches, particularly because of the life-conferring power of the sacraments, most of which are usually administered by the clergy — especially baptism, which initiates spiritual life in the soul.

If priests were to accept that title pridefully, rather than with the emphasis on the responsibility it entails, they would be violating the purpose of Jesus' injunction. When people ask me if they must call me Father, I reply that they may call me anything except late for breakfast.

How do I tell Protestant friends that the Catholic use of statues is not idolatry?

Idolatry is a terrible sin, condemned by God in countless Old Testament passages, and in the New Testament also (e.g. 1 Pet. 4:3 and 1 Jn. 5:21), for it is giving to a material thing that which belongs to God alone, namely adoration or worship. "My glory I will not give to another, nor my praise to idols" (Is. 42:8).

Not just Catholics but also many Protestants use statues on church lawns, in cemeteries, etc., or stained-glass windows of Jesus with the Apostles, etc., but there is no idolatry there, of course. There are statues of war heroes, patriots, etc., in many parks, but not for idolatrous use. In the rotunda of our nation's capitol, there are statues of our country's founding fathers, but no idolatry. The great statue of Lincoln in the Lincoln Memorial is the scene of civil and religious gatherings, but there is no idolatry there. Images on stamps, coins, and currency, or framed on classroom walls evoke no idolatry, any more than wallet photos, teddy bears or bronzed baby shoes. Museums are full of images and statues without idolatry. If all graven images were intrinsically evil, it would be a sin for a Christian to become a sculptor.

One lady I know complained to me of my use of statues as idolatrous while she chatted with me in her living room; on the coffee table in front of her was her own nativity scene made of small statues. She was indignant when I humorously accused her of idolatry. We Catholics use statues, paintings, holy cards, stained-glass images, etc. as reminders of God's heroes, such as those extolled in Hebrews 11, but we especially honor Christ by such images. To worship such an image would certainly be idolatry; to use them as forms of inspiration and prayer-focus draws us closer to God, not causing us to turn from him as idolatry would. As in all Catholic practices, there is a biblical support for proper use of statues and images, as Moses used the bronze serpent displayed on a pole (Num. 21:8), or Paul's reference to a crucifix (Gal. 3:1). Solomon used sculptured cherubs in the temple (2 Chron. 3:7, 10); even on the ark of the covenant there were "graven images" of cherubim (Exod. 25:18; 37:7) and in the sanctuary (Ezek. 41:25; 1 Kings 6:23, 27; 8:7; Heb. 9:5).

Does the Bible forbid the use of statues for religious purposes?

Statues and carved (graven) images are not forbidden by the Bible, but worshiping or adoring them certainly is. God himself commanded that graven images be made, as when he told Moses to make a bronze serpent for people to look upon to be healed from snakebite (Num. 21:8), or when God commanded images to be carved for his Ark of the Covenant in the tabernacle (Ex. 25:18, 37:7) and embroidered on cloth (26:2, 31). He commanded statues of angels to be placed in the Holy of Holies (Heb. 9:5; 2 Chron. 3:10) in Solomon's temple, and carved on doors and walls, with human and lion faces (Ezek. 41:19). He even gave names to two pillars at the front of the temple (2 Chron. 3:17). Twelve metal oxen stood in the temple (4:4) and panels of carved lions, bulls, and cherubim (1 Kings 7:29). So the Bible not only allows but encourages statues, but not idols — that is, statues to be worshiped, as Is. 42:8 indicates.

Catholic Teaching

What is the "just war theory"?

The just-war theory holds that any given war can be "just" on only one side, if at all — as in the case of a burglar and a self-defending victim. Theoretically, both sides can't be fighting an objectively "just" war. Certain conditions would *always* be required to make it "just" or justified on that one side. With modern weaponry, many ethicians doubt that *all* of these conditions can ever actually be fulfilled in typical international conflicts today. Vatican II (*Gaudium et Spes*, art. 80) says "All these factors force us to undertake a completely fresh reappraisal of war." Pope John XXIII, in his encyclical *Pacem in Terris*, wrote, "In this age . . . of atomic power, it is irrational to think that war is a proper way to obtain justice for violated rights."

For permitting a "just war," different ethicians list different conditions, but the following list of nine conditions is perhaps representative of the thinking of the most astute ethicians:

1) The goal or cause of the war must be just, such as deterring or repelling aggression, or righting a grievous wrong.

2) The intention of engaging in war must be just or "right," such as preventing an enormous disaster or defending against a great injury.

3) The principle of proportionality must be applicable to the goal. That is, the good to be attained or maintained by the war must be commensurate or proportionate to the evils of death, devastation, etc., that result from war.

4) The same principle of proportionality must be applicable to the means used. For instance, it would be using a disproportionate and therefore unjust means to a given end to use indiscriminate terrorism, or to cause a large ecologically

destructive oil spill designed to slow down a sea attack, or to bomb an entire village to wipe out a hidden anti-aircraft nest. (It is this principle that brings into question the morality of nuclear, biological, and chemical warfare, ecological and climate-control warfare, etc.)

5) The war must be the absolutely last resort to solving the conflict; that is, only after all other means of diplomacy, reasonable compromise, etc. have proven unsuccessful.

6) There must be a reasonable prospect of success in pursuing the (just) goal of the war. (To enter a war with certainty of failure would be to induce needless misery.)

7) The war must be undertaken by legitimate authority, not simply a gang of rebels with narrow group goals, unrepresentative of the commonweal or general welfare.

8) When possible, enemy personnel must be captured rather than killed, and treated humanely as prisoners of war.

9) The immunity of noncombatants and their resources (water supplies, etc.) must be respected; any deaths, injury or hardships of noncombatants ("collateral damage") must be incidental and not directly intended, even though perhaps foreseen.

Both during and after every war there is much heated debate (and much conjecture beforehand) about whether all these principles are in fact applicable. Many questions of fact cannot be settled until long after the war's end — such as the question of long-term peace being advanced or set back by the war, the long-range aftereffects on a homeless and war-displaced populace, resultant economic deficits, etc.

The geopolitical issues and seemingly abstract ethical questions can seem almost irrelevant in the face of human tragedy resulting from any war. The real answer to the dreadful war issue is to be found in those who work for and pray for peace, for as James says (3:18), "Peacemakers who sow in peace raise a harvest of righteousness." Or, in the beatitudinal promise of Jesus (Mt. 5:9), "Blessed are the peacemakers, for they will be called children of God."

What are the seven gifts of the Holy Spirit?

The seven gifts of the Holy Spirit are called personal or "sanctificatory" gifts; they are mentioned in Isaiah 11:2-3 as qualities of the Messiah who was to come. Actually, only six gifts are listed there, but the last one, fear of the Lord, is mentioned twice under different aspects; its first occurrence is translated as "piety" in the Septuagint and Vulgate versions; this accounts for the traditional Catholic listing of seven gifts: wisdom, understanding, knowledge, counsel, fortitude, piety and fear of the Lord.

During the age of monasticism, when contemplative prayer was highlighted in the Church, the seven personal gifts of the Spirit were encouraged while the charismatic gifts were downplayed, because of abuses that had crept in — similar to those of the Corinthians that Paul had to correct; for though they did not "lack any spiritual gift" (1 Cor. 1:7), they were ignorant of their proper use (12:1). Various listings of the charismatic gifts are found in Mark 16:17-18; Romans 12:6-8; 1 Corinthians 12:8-10; Ephesians 4:11 and 1 Peter 4:11.

These sublime "sanctificatory" gifts are refinements of the life of virtue, enhancing the holiness of the individual, which is characterized by the fruit of the Spirit (Gal. 5:22-23).

What is Church teaching about reincarnation?

Reincarnation (also called soul-transmigration or metempsychosis) is a belief in a succession of rebirths — a tenet generally rejected by Jewish, Christian, and Muslim theology. It originated probably in India in the sixth century B.C. and became popularized in the West as an import from Eastern religions, especially Hinduism and Buddhism, whose teachings in this matter are quite similar to each other. Adherents are urged to seek to ascend by the law of karma toward the nirvana state, which entails either the extinction of all desires and passions or the extinction of individuality by one's atman or individual spirit. Some reincarnationists teach endless recycling of human life. Others believe that each entity ascends or descends the ladder of life, even into and out of animal states, depending on how each life is lived. (One henpecked husband said that if his wife came back as a dog, he would return as a flea.)

The only "reincarnation" that a Christian may profess is that which takes place at the time of the second coming of Jesus, when the soul of each deceased person will be reembodied — "reincarnated," so to speak — in its own (one) body, newly resurrected and "spiritualized." Paul writes: "So it will be with the resurrection of the dead . . . sown [buried] a natural body, it is raised a spiritual body" (1 Cor. 15:42-44). This and other Scripture passages clearly imply that each soul has its own body which will be spiritualized and will not reanimate another body with another personality.

If a soul had previously belonged to a succession of bodies, which one would it be joined with at the resurrection? Would its many former bodies then remain soulless, with their personhood forever extinct? Or would the one soul be shared with its multiple bodies simultaneously?

Paul tells us that before the living the dead will be "raptured" or "caught up" with the Lord at his Second Coming (1 Thess. 4:15-17). Would one's former (dead) bodies need to recapture the soul from the living body in order to be raptured first, thus killing that person? If so, how could that same body be later raptured without its own soul? Would one's many former (dead) bodies compete for their one soul?

Or consider this conundrum: Daniel prophesied (12:2) that at the time of the future great tribulation, "many of those who sleep in the dust of the earth shall awake: some to everlasting life, and some to shame and everlasting contempt." Jesus reiterated this prophecy of the resurrection of both good and evil persons, to salvation and damnation respectively (Jn. 5:29). What would be the fate of a soul that has animated a succession

61

of many bodies, some as good persons, some as bad? Would such a soul have multiple destinies of salvation and damnation?

Reincarnation teaches that one must pay for one's sins by struggles through successive incarnations. Christianity teaches that no one can reach salvation by one's own effort (Eph. 2:8-9; Rom. 3:24; 4:2, 2 Tim. 1:9), and that Jesus alone brings expiation for sin: "Salvation is found in no one else" (Acts 4:12).

What is the Church teaching about purgatory?

In a cemetery in Ohio there is a tombstone with a classical epitaph that reads: "Too bad for heaven, too good for hell; where he went I cannot tell."

In a facetious way, that simple epitaph provides a framework for an understanding of purgatory. "Too bad for heaven" is another way of saying what Scripture says in Revelation 21:27, namely, that nothing defiled can enter heaven. The phrase "too good for hell" reaffirms the assertion of 1 John 5:16-17, that "all wrongdoing is sin, and there is sin that does not lead to [spiritual] death."

Such non-damning sins on one's soul, unrepented at the time of death, need to be "purged" by some purging or purgatorial cleansing after death. Any soul thus "defiled" must become "undefiled" to enter heaven, as required by Rev. 21:27. For instance, a dying person who does not totally and lovingly accept deathbed suffering and the consequent death as God's will would have some degree of "defilement" because of that nonconformity with God's will. That sin or fault would have to be purged before that soul could enter the awesome presence of the all-holy Godhead. Also deep-seated habits or thought patterns reflecting insensitivity to sin, like impatience, habits of gossip, resentment, etc., need to be purified.

Thus, purgatory is a school of relearning, in which souls are fully trained in the ways of God that they neglected to learn during life. And, incidental to this spiritual training, there is suffering, for we must "endure hardship as discipline" (Heb. 12:7).

But Scripture speaks of a second dynamic involved in this purgation, namely that of bringing to perfection one's earthly activities or "works." As Paul reminds us, "We must all appear before the judgment seat of Christ, that each one may receive what is due him for the things done while in the body, whether good or bad" (2 Cor. 5:10). He also describes the person whose works fall short of God's testing: "he himself will be saved, but only as one escaping through the flames" (1 Cor. 3:15). Such righteous persons have their salvation assured, but they must go through a fiery purifying experience first, like gold or silver purified of its dross by the refiner's fire (Mal. 3:2-3, etc.), fire being a scriptural symbol of purification (e.g., 1 Pet. 1:7).

There are many "hints" also in the Old Testament about this "escape" or "release" of the dead from some kind of bondage. To quote only a few: "He [the Lord] frees us! He delivers us from death" (Ps 68:20 LB). Psalm 56:13 says: "You have saved me from death . . . so that I can walk before God in the land of the living." This thought is reasserted in 1 Samuel 2:6, in a quote from Hannah's song: "The Lord kills, The Lord gives life" (releases us). Yet no release is required for those who die in true holiness: "The righteous man . . . enters into peace; they rest in their beds who walk in their uprightness" (Is. 57:1-2).

The flames that Paul speaks of we know very little about, as Pope Paul VI stated. But, as St. Thomas Aquinas said in his commentary on 1 Cor. 3:15, purgatorial fire, unlike hellfire, is purifying rather than afflictive. It is the flame of God's love (Song of Songs: 8:6) that builds up the soul's undeveloped love capacity. It's a beautiful inflaming of God's love that makes the soul yearn for him with an intensity that is beyond description, and its cleansing effect is a kind of "baptism at the entrance of paradise," as St. Ambrose describes it. The intense suffering is simply the unfulfilled longing for God, a painful love —

yearning for God, who is poignantly recognized immediately after death as the be-all and end-all of one's very existence.

Summarizing the declarations of the Second Council of Nicea in 787 and the Council of Florence in 1439, the Council of Trent (1549-63) declared: "There is a purgatory, and the souls detained there are helped by the 'suffrages' [i.e., the prayers and sacrifices] of the faithful." These two facts, stated simply in one sentence, embrace the entire official teaching of the Catholic Church on purgatory. Praying for the dead must never be an attempt to communicate with them by necromancy, as in a seance, which is a sin forbidden by the Church on eight occasions, and also by the Bible (Deut. 18:10-12). Yet "it was a holy and pious thought [to pray in] atonement for the dead, that they might be delivered from their sin" (2 Mac. 12:46).

The "suffering" of purgatory is very real, and is twofold: a profound remorse for sin and a profound longing for the fullness of God's presence (Beatific Vision: 1 Cor. 13:12). The purpose of this "suffering" is also twofold: first, a purification from the defilement of any unrepented venial sin (and this could conceivably be done in an instant, at the moment the soul separates from the body, when it clearly recognizes the heinousness of sin and repents); and second, a perfecting or spiritual growth process in undeveloped virtue, especially love, along with disengagement from long habits of sin and long-standing thought patterns like resentments, etc. We know that post-death learning and improvement is possible because Jesus evangelized deceased persons (1 Pet. 3:19 and 4:6) between Good Friday and Easter Sunday.

How can one be sure that "prophecy" given by an individual is genuine?

Observations from the Scripture and Vatican II documents imply that a certain discernment is necessary to "weigh carefully what is said" (1 Cor. 14:29). In this matter another charism is helpful — that of discernment of spirits (1 Cor. 12:10) to "test the spirits" (1 Jn. 4:1). Underlying this Spirit-activated charism of discernment are several norms of discerning the authenticity of any prophecy:

1) In any authentic prophecy most of those present, especially if they are baptized in the Spirit, will experience what is called the "witness of the Spirit" — an inner response that recognizes the presence and action of God in the utterance of the prophecy. 2) In the case of the more rare predictive type of prophecy (as in Acts 21:10, where Agabus predicts Paul's future imprisonment), the prophecy must be fulfilled to be authentic (Deut. 18:22). However, sometimes a futuristic prophecy is an expression of God's conditional will, as St. Thomas Aquinas says, and such a prophecy may be authentic but not fulfilled because of intervening conditions, as when Isaiah told Hezekiah he was near death but Hezekiah's prayers led God to relent and extend his life fifteen years (2 Kings 20:1-7; 2 Chron 32:24; Is. 38:1-5). In the same way, many private revelations of doom and disaster given in publicized visions, etc., are conditional, dependent on widespread refusal to pray, fast, etc. Another example of this reversal of prophecy is seen in Jonah 3:10.

3) Authentic prophecies will never state anything that contravenes Scripture, since God will not contradict what he has already revealed about himself. (Sometimes shared Scripture passages in the same meeting will coincide with authentic prophecies.) Neither will authentic prophecies contravene tradition of basic Christian teachings (2 Thess. 2:15; Jude 3; 2 Tim. 1:13-14; 3:14).

4) Several persons may receive essentially the same message simultaneously, although only one may speak it. This faith-building experience, called "confirmation of a prophecy," usually affirms the authenticity of the prophecy by way of "supernatural coincidence" and is a rather common experience in mature groups of charismatics.

5) An essential sign for the person giving the prophecy to

establish its authenticity is the "anointing" — that is, the inner prompting or urging from the Spirit to speak. For the less experienced person, this prompting is usually weak, but it grows stronger with use over a period of time, until a person with the gift of prophecy acquires a ministry of prophecy and thus becomes a "prophet," recognized as such by the community. The deeper the "anointing" the more of God and the less of self comes through the prophetic words.

6) In line with the discernment principles of St. John of the Cross, prophetic utterance can have its origin in any of three sources: God (good), a demonic source (bad), or self (neutral). Thus the Holy Spirit gives true prophecy, the evil spirit causes false prophecy, and the human spirit causes "non-prophecy" "By their fruits you shall know them," said Jesus (Mt. 7:16).

7) The community discernment takes precedence over the individual discernment of the one prophesying, as St. Ignatius says. Anyone arrogantly refusing to accept this norm should not be recognized by the community (see 1 Cor. 14:36-38).

In spite of the fact that false prophecy from the evil one is quite rare (like a demonically inspired gift of tongues), still Jesus advises caution: "Watch out for false prophets. They come to you in sheep's clothing, but inwardly they are ferocious wolves" (Mt. 7:15). "Many will say to me on that day, 'Lord, Lord, did we not prophesy in your name. . . ?' I will tell them plainly, I never knew you. Away from me, you evildoers!" (vss. 22-23). Those rejected by Jesus on judgment day are those who only ostensibly act in his name and do not do "the will of the Father in heaven" (vs. 21) by sincerely submitting their heart to the Lord. Prophesying in Christ's name avails them nothing because they seek to establish their own righteousness rather than God's (Rom. 10:3), and do not offer themselves to God "as instruments of righteousness" (6:13).

The entire prayer group, and especially the leader and the pastor, must strive to safeguard the purity of the sacred charisms like prophecy. Vatican II speaks of this in two places.

Referring to extraordinary gifts (like publicized prophetic visions, etc.) the Constitution on the Church, art. 12 states, "Judgment as to their genuineness and proper use belongs to those who preside over the Church, and to those whose special competence it belongs, not indeed to extinguish the Spirit, but to test all things and hold fast to that which is good" (see 1 Thess. 5:12, 19-21). We are commanded in Hebrews 13:17: "Obey your leaders and submit to their authority. They keep watch over you as men who must give an account." Thus, a leader or pastor who quenches the Spirit by rashness will have to render an account to God. But anyone who refuses to submit to proper leadership will also have to render an account of such disobedience.

The decree on the Apostolate of the Laity, in referring to the use of charismatic gifts for the welfare of the Church (art. 3), reaffirms the same idea, while showing the compatibility of discernment with spiritual freedom: "Believers need to enjoy the freedom of the Holy Spirit who breathes where he wills (Jn. 3:8). At the same time, they must act in communion with their brothers and sisters in Christ, and especially with their pastors. The latter must make a judgment about the true nature and proper use of these gifts, not in order to extinguish the Spirit, but to test all things and hold fast to what is good."

Christian History

How were years numbered before the creation of the Christian calendar when the enumeration of years as "A.D." or "B.C." began?

Taking year 1 as the year of the birth of Christ, and creating from that a universal time counting for history, was the magnificent undertaking of a monk of the sixth century by the name of Dionysius Exiguus, meaning "Dennis the Small." He started the movement to replace the ancient enumeration of years, which was based on a counting from the foundation of Rome, regarded as the center of civilization. So for the first six centuries or so of our Christian era, historians didn't count from the birth of Christ; later historians transposed any historical dating of those early centuries to the Christian-era formulation.

Dionysius used the beginning of Jesus' public life as a historical platform from which to calculate the year of his birth. He used the phrase from Luke 3:23, "about thirty years of age" for this purpose. Unfortunately, he paid too little regard to the word "about," and as a result his reckoning was probably four to seven years off the mark, so that Jesus was really born in "B.C." — "before Christ"!

The universal Christian influence was so great that eventually even non-Christian countries began to measure historical dates for the "year of the Lord" even though they didn't accept Christ as their Lord. Countries today must be a bit embarrassed by being historically compelled to use a calendar counting from the birth of Christ, whom they don't acknowledge as special.

Jewish historians, archeologists, etc., use the initials "C.E.," meaning "Common Era," to coincide their enumerations with the Christian calendar. "C.E." can also mean "Christian Era."

"B.C.E. (Before the Christian Era)" is acceptable to them, since it doesn't refer to the Lordship of Jesus as "A.D." does in its Latin equivalent, "year of the Lord."

Everyday Ethics

Isn't it immoral to hunt animals, trap them, or subject them to pain in laboratory experimentation?

Aside from the animals-as-food issue — the vegetarian controversy — there is the "vivisectionist" controversy — a very complex issue in itself. Starting with the basic principle that "a righteous man cares for the needs of his animals" (Prov. 12:10), it is obviously "unrighteous" or immoral to cause any animal *needless* suffering. In animal experimentation for the advance of medicine, surgery, etc., such needless suffering could be caused by not using analgesics or anesthetics for animals being tested in painful procedures, using repetitive procedures for already proven conclusions to maintain a government or private grant, subjecting animals to extreme or prolonged pain for relatively superficial reasons, such as testing the safety of luxury cosmetics, etc. Certainly any practice of sadism would be outrageous and clearly immoral. All induced animal suffering must be done only as a last resort, and with a proportionately good effect reasonably foreseen.

Using animals for sports would fit into the same principle of proportionality. In general there is little abuse in horse racing, somewhat more in dog racing. Pheasant or deer hunting, especially in overstocked areas, would be permissible where every effort is used to make the kill "humanely." Morally questionable practices would include painful animal trapping (with sometimes days of agony for a trapped animal), trapping for luxury furs, bullfighting, cockfighting, pit-bull dogfighting, etc., for gambling purposes.

The African elephant is nearing extinction because of ivory poachers who kill them only for the tusks — even baby elephants. (During the 1980s three-fourths of the African elephant population had been wantonly slaughtered.) This is not even sport and is obviously immoral, as is also buying ivory and thus supporting this illegal and sinful practice.

Seriously immoral acts would include satanic animal sacrifice, animal torture, ritualistic or otherwise, or occultic animal slaughter, as in Santeria practices, etc.

In spite of the norms for kindness to animals, there are times when pain may be inflicted on them for a good reason. God commanded Joshua (Josh. 11:6) to hamstring hundreds of chariot horses of Israel's enemies (cutting the tendon above the hock or ankle to cripple them) as a way of immobilizing these animals used as instruments of war. Likewise David hamstrung hundreds of Hadadezer's chariot horses for the same reason (1 Chron. 18:4, 2 Sam. 8:4). Yet Simon and Levi were repudiated by Jacob (Gen. 49:6-7) for wantonly doing the same thing to oxen. Thus any act can be moral or immoral, depending on the circumstances. In the case of Joshua and David, the God-directed act was not a vicious act of wanton cruelty as it was in the case of Simon and Levi, but an act of war in attacking an enemy and its equipment, which happened to be animals, just as tanks and even humans are targets of attack in modern warfare. Again, inflicting needless pain on animals is contrary to God's will.

Balaam's donkey was beaten three times by his anger-motivated master, and God allowed the animal to speak in a human voice to show Balaam by this miracle that he was doing something immoral, for which he repented (Num. 22:34). Yet he went on from there to slaughter seven bulls and seven rams as a sacrifice for the Lord (23:2). Here we see in the same person an improper use of an animal, by abuse, and a proper use of animals by religious sacrifice. In both cases there was some pain to animals (although Jewish law requires truly humane slaughter in sacrificial killings). So, as in the parallel case of proper and improper pain-causing by hamstringing, we again see that circumstances can determine the morality or immorality of causing pain to animals.

Of course, animals may be tamed (James 3:7), and also trained, as for circus use, animals shows and contests, etc., but of course without unnecessary confinement or suffering. Seeing-eye dogs experience restriction, but not excessively so, usually. The same is true of most zoo animals.

As creatures of God, don't animals have the same rights as human beings?

That's not quite correct. Otherwise you couldn't exterminate cockroaches or termites, or kill a poisonous snake in your yard, or "put to sleep" an old arthritic dog or sick cat; nor could you go fishing or hunting, or work in a slaughterhouse killing animals for food; you couldn't euthanize a horse with a broken leg, nor could you swat a fly, nor destroy aphids or snails in your garden. You would have to forgo eating chicken, turkey, fish, lard, beef, pork, most soups, broths, etc., etc. Carrying this to its ultimate conclusion, you would not be allowed to kill germs with disinfectants, nor bacteria with antibiotics. And you could not wear leather shoes or belts.

If animals had rights like humans, then to kill an animal for such reasons would be murder, and that of course is absurd. Animals have souls, of course, but not spiritual souls with the Godlike qualities of intellect and will, as we humans have. For this reason, says St. Thomas Aquinas, they don't have rights as we do; neutered animals, for instance, would not be deprived of a "right" to have offspring. They have some "rights" in the broad sense of that word, since they are the handiwork of God. St. Francis of Assisi called them his "brothers and sisters," as he so famously related to all animals with love — an admirable attitude that you seem to have also.

God has designed a subordination in his creation, so that a prey-and-predator dynamic is operative: big fish eat little fish, lions eat antelopes, etc. At the top of this hierarchical pyramid is mankind by God's specific design: "God said . . . 'Rule over the fish of the sea and the birds of the air and over every living creature. . .' " (Gen. 1:28). To Noah God said, "Every moving thing that lives shall be food for you; and as I gave you the green plants, I give you everything" (9:3). "You made man ruler over the works of your hands; you put everything under his feet" (Ps. 8:6).

Under Mosaic law God specified that for his chosen people, some animals as food were "clean" and some "unclean" (Lev. 11 and Deut. 14), although this didn't apply to "foreigners" (Deut. 14:21). In Christian times, all food was made kosher by God (Acts 10:15). If animals may be used legitimately for food, then they may also be used as donors for body parts or biochemical needs for humans, and also for clothing such as wool, leather, etc. (Lev. 13:48).

Domestic pets are one of God's most precious gifts to mankind, and can bring great pleasure to their owners. The pet dog of Tobias was mentioned four times in the book of Tobit — even his delightful romping and tail-wagging (11:9).

In general, kindness to animals is demanded by God's law (Ex. 23:4), and it is rewarded by him. God even promises a long life to those showing special kindness to birds (Deut. 22:6-7). And Jesus himself pointed out that even the Sabbath laws could be suspended to assist a helpless animal (Lk. 14:5).

I hope that your love for animals will extend to praying for animals being abused and tortured all over the world, as one should pray for humans being abused in so many ways. Some owners bless their pets daily with holy water for health and safety. May the great exemplar of the virtue of loving animals, St. Francis, by his intercession, call down God's blessings on you for loving and protecting God's precious creatures.

God

Isn't war totally unacceptable to God?

Undoubtedly war is the primary evidence of the evil that pervades humanity as a result, ultimately, of original sin. War in general has been repeatedly condemned by popes, bishops, statesmen, kings, editors, generals, and the man on the street. Yet, through the centuries it continues in many places in the world at any given time. And eschatological prophecies affirm that "to the end there shall be war" (Dan. 9:26).

Apparently, in certain circumstances, war is justified. The Bible records many wars fought by God's chosen people with the Lord's backing. For instance, in his sovereignty over human life, God supported and guided Joshua in his bloody wars with the many countries that opposed the Israelites' acquisition of lands allotted to them by a special providence (see Josh. 10-13). And Saul was rejected by God as king of Israel because he didn't completely destroy every single Amalekite and their cattle in war as God commanded (1 Sam. 15).

In spite of such God-supported warfare, it seems God does not condone war *in general*. Proverbs 16:32 says: "Better to have self-control than to control an army." David was not allowed to build the temple he planned, said the Lord, because he "fought great wars and shed much blood on earth" (1 Chron. 22:8), while his son Solomon was assigned by God to build the temple because he was to be a man of peace (verse 9). Yet David prayed for peace: "Scatter the peoples who delight in war," he sang (Ps. 68:30).

When precisely is war seen as acceptable to God? That is, when is war justified? The answer to this difficult and age-old question evolved over the centuries into the so-called "just-war" theory described today in the science of ethics and

74

moral theology. It was perhaps first formulated by St. Augustine in the fourth century, and refined by St. Thomas Aquinas in the thirteenth century, and also by Francisco de Vitoria. Hugo Grotius developed its present generally exposited form (see page 58).

Why does a "good" God allow innocent people to suffer and wicked people to prosper?

If you read the book of Job in the Bible, I'm sure you can identify with his suffering and the persecution he endured. But there's so much else that would clear up your confusion, such as God giving permission to Satan twice to wreak harm on Job (1:12 and 2:6), because God foresaw the good that would ultimately eventuate from the trials that Satan would cause Job. But in spite of Job's complaints to God and his disclaimers to his three accusers, Job never stopped trusting God: "Though he slay me, yet will I trust him" (13:15). The bottom line of the terrible ordeal of having his ten children killed and all his property lost along with his health, etc., was the insight into the meaning of suffering that he was given in chapter 42: "I have uttered what I did not understand, things too wonderful for me, which I did not know . . . but now my eye sees you; therefore I despise myself, and repent" (42:3-6). Most of your theological confusion would be dissolved if you carefully and prayerfully read and studied the book of Job.

The holocaust, with all its horror (and punishment for any unrepentant perpetrators), was not without many far-reaching good consequences, too numerous to mention — not the least of which was the establishment of the state of Israel in 1948. God did not turn a deaf ear to the cries of the holocaust victims; the Lord anguished for them more than they did for themselves, but he will not interfere with the free will of humans — even malicious humans. He then proceeds to make good come from the evil actions of humans, as in the case of Paul, who rejoiced in his imprisonment and torture because he knew it would ultimately turn out for his good (Phil. 1:19). For the good persons who suffer and the evil ones who cause it, there are corresponding sanctions — often in this life in countless ways, and certainly also in the next: "Those who have done good will rise to live, and those who have done evil will rise to be condemned (Jn. 5:29).

Jesus, as a human, was repelled by suffering and asked that the cup of suffering be removed, but conditioned that request with a prayer of submission to his Father, "May your will be done." The epistle of Hebrews comments on this: "During the days of Jesus' life on earth, he offered up prayers and petitions with loud cries and tears to the one who could save him from death [like the holocaust victims, etc.], *and he was heard because of his reverent submission*" (Heb. 5:7). His prayer was heard, not by being saved from death, but by being saved *out* of death by resurrection — a prototype of our own resurrection into a super-blissful eternal life. The prayers of holocaust victims, and others suffering as Jesus did, will likewise not go unheard.

But other catastrophes, such as floods and earthquakes that do not result from human malice, can also ultimately redound to good. However, in any kind of suffering, there are two conditions, says Paul, for all things to work together for good: one must truly love God, and must fit into his plan, i.e., respond "according to his purpose" (Rom. 8:28). Loving God and not rebelling against his will (even his permissive will that allows evil) are responses to love and trust that God uses to "draw straight with crooked lines," as the Portuguese proverb has it.

Paul, who suffered so much unjustly, was given inspired insight that put the whole matter of suffering in perspective eschatologically: "I consider that our present sufferings are *not worth comparing* with the glory that will be revealed in us [heavenly reward]" (Rom. 8:18); "for our . . . momentary troubles are achieving for us an *eternal glory that far outweighs them all*" (2 Cor. 4:17). Peter's words are equally

76

perspicacious: "Dear friends, do not be surprised at the painful trial you are suffering, as though something strange were happening to you. But rejoice that you participate in the sufferings of Christ, so that you may be overjoyed when his glory is revealed" (1 Pet. 4:12-13).

Sinners don't "have the best of life," although *some* have more luxuries than holy persons. In spite of material luxury, "there is no peace, says my God, for the wicked" (Is. 57:21), but "He will keep in perfect peace *all those who trust in him*, whose thoughts turn often to the Lord!" (Is. 26:3). Besides, the luxury question becomes meaningless in view of the definitive statement of Jesus: The wicked "will go away to eternal punishment, but the righteous to eternal life" (Mt. 25:46).

The devil doesn't cause all our suffering, although he does cause much of it, as the book of Job proves. Being the "prince of this world" does not make Satan more powerful than Christ, for "the prince of this world will be driven out," Jesus said (Jn. 12:31), and that will happen by means of his own redemptive suffering (vss. 32-33). "The reason the Son of God appeared was to destroy the devil's work" (1 Jn. 3:8).

If God is truly merciful, why would there be a need for purgatory?

More than five hundred Scripture passages refer to God's mercy in forgiving repented sin, such as Hebrews 8:12: "I will forgive their wickedness and will remember their sins no more." The Catholic Church champions the teaching on God's mercy (a part of which is purgatory itself, paradoxically). Purgatory does not cause the removal of sin, as many non-Catholics accuse us of teaching. Purgatory clears up only the effects of that forgiven sin. Jesus' blood shed on Calvary purifies us of sin (1 Jn. 1:7, etc.), but not necessarily of the remnant effects of that sin — such as the tendency or habit of sin. Jesus' redemptive act does not "cancel the acquired propensity to evil," as St. Gregory of Nyssa wrote in the fourth century. Yet, by God's mercy and grace we can work toward that supplementary goal, as the Bible so often attests, toward a fuller purification (1 Pet. 1:22), and a completing of a salvation already attained by faith (vs. 5).

If we don't do this completely in this life, it will have to be done in the next, as St. Augustine reminds us. In this regard, Jesus' words in Matthew 5:25-26 are appropriate: "Settle matters quickly . . . do it while you are still on the way . . . or you may be thrown into prison. I tell you the truth, you will not get out until you have paid the last penny." This specifies and reaffirms what Jesus spoke of elsewhere (Mt. 18:34), in terms of debt payment for moral failure of the unjust steward, who was jailed "until he should pay back all that was owed."

Overall, the lessons of purgatory are encouraging: First, because its purification (not punishment) is a form of suffering that is intensely love-inflamed; second, it teaches us that we can accomplish the same purgation painlessly here on earth; and third, it teaches us that we have, by God's goodness, a powerful means at our disposal to assist souls now in purgatory who are pleading for our help by our prayers.

Why does God create people he knows will be condemned?

Your question, when left unanswered, has led countless persons into atheism through the centuries. It's the classic challenge to the whole concept of theology. Perhaps that's why Paul dealt with that question at length, especially in Romans 8 and 9, while often referring in his epistles to the concept of "election" or predestination.

Clearly, God "wants *all* men to be saved" (1 Tim. 2:4). "He is patient with you, not wanting *anyone* to perish, but *everyone* to come to repentance" (2 Pet. 3:9). The Calvinistic theology that maintains that some persons are irreversibly predestined to heaven and some to hell was a tenet that had been condemned in the Council of Mainz in 848, several centuries before Calvin proposed it.

Yet the Bible teaches that there is such a thing as predestination on God's part. Predestination embraces the heavenly reward intended by God for *all* humans, as well as the grace-dispensing that will lead to that reward. Prescience, or foreknowledge, on God's part is connected with but distinct from this predestination.

Those God *foreknew* he also *predestined . . .* and those he called he also *justified*; those he justified he also *glorified* (Rom. 8:29-30).

Paul follows this with the example of the Pharaoh of the Exodus, whose heart God "hardened" in evil, after having offered him multiple opportunities to comply with the divine plan presented by Moses. God *foreknew* or foresaw the refusal to comply (Ex. 3:19). In view of that foreseen refusal, God would harden Pharaoh's heart, but only *after* Pharaoh had hardened his own heart by his first refusal. In this sense it can be said that God "predestined" him to evil, and to the consequence of that evil. Paul concludes, "Therefore God has mercy on whom he wants to have mercy, and he hardens whom he wants to harden" (Rom. 9:18).

At this point he anticipates the burning question, "Then why does God still blame us?" (vs. 19). That is to say, if God chooses to create two kinds of people, the elect and the reprobate, and programs them to respond accordingly, doesn't he then accept the responsibility for the sin of the sinner as well as the virtue of the just? Doesn't this make God the author of sin as well as the author of grace?

This conclusion runs counter to Scripture: "You are not a God who gets pleasure from wickedness" (Ps. 5:4); "Your eyes are too pure to look on evil; you cannot tolerate wrong" (Hab. 1:13). "God cannot be tempted by evil, nor does he tempt anyone" (Jas. 1:13). How then do we explain the apparent contradiction?

On what basis has God chosen his elect? Certainly not on the basis of any merit on their part (Eph. 2:8-9); but they were chosen "in him [Christ]" (Eph. 1:4); the Father chooses those who are in his Son, Jesus, that is, united to him by faith. But what determines that faith, by which, for instance, one person responds to an altar call while another refuses? Jesus seems to answer that question in John 6:37: "All that the Father gives to me will come to me, and whoever comes to me I will never drive away." This means that there is nothing in the principle of "election" or predestination that will keep any repentant sinner from coming to Christ and receiving salvation.

However, in John 6:44 Jesus also said, "No one can come to me unless the Father who sent me draws him." Those who come to Christ do so as a result of the working of God in their hearts; it is God the Father who draws them to God the Son, their Savior. A father may bestow or withhold an inheritance on the basis of the child's *foreseeable* use or misuse of it. Likewise, God's grace is dispensed on the basis of his infallible foreknowledge of our use or misuse of that grace.

Hence, whoever rejects the Lord Jesus must bear all the blame for remaining condemned (non-elect), just as those who are saved must give God all the glory.

Jesus

What can be said to defend the belief that Jesus truly rose from the dead?

One of the best foundational proofs of the divinity of Christ, is his prophecy of his own resurrection.

Imagine your reaction to someone who would make claims like, "No person can come to God except through me," or "Believe in me and I will give you eternal life," or "I will forgive your sins," or "Ask anything in my name and I will give it to you." You would regard such a person as either a lunatic or a super con artist. But if he could back up such claims, your only other alternative would be to acknowledge this person as God himself in human form.

Either Jesus was God, capable of fulfilling his claims, or he was a lunatic or con artist. This binary choice — Jesus is either God or a charlatan — is contingent on whether or not he rose from the dead as he promised. Jesus made these claims and promised to back them up by rising from death to life after being entombed for three days. The conclusion: Christianity, founded by this Jesus, must be either true or false, based on whether or not its leader fulfilled these promises.

"If Christ has not been raised, our preaching is useless and so is your faith . . . we are then found to be false witnesses about God. . . . If Christ has not been raised, your faith is futile; you are still in your sins . . . [and] those who have fallen asleep in Christ are lost" (1 Cor. 15:14-18).

Even the great skeptic and rationalist Wilhelm DeWette, after the most precise and scientific investigation, claimed that the certainty of Christ's resurrection paralleled the historical certainty of the assassination of Julius Caesar, one of the most thoroughly documented events of early history.

Circumstantial evidence supplements the physical evidence of the Resurrection. For instance, something very significant must have happened that first day of the week to induce the Apostles to change their lifelong Jewish practice of Sabbath observance to Sunday observance as a norm for Christians after that time.

There is no doubt that on Easter morning the tomb was empty (except for the linen wrappings — which would probably have been taken with the body if it had been stolen). The chief priests' efforts to create a "stolen body" story and the bribery of the tomb guards to support it (Mt. 28:12-13) would have been unnecessary if Jesus' body were obviously in the tomb. Also it would have been needless to attempt to conceal any events from Pilate (vs. 14).

If then the tomb was empty on Sunday morning, could the disciples have stolen the body? It was precisely because the chief priests and Pharisees had suspected such a plot on the part of the disciples that they determined to prevent it by obtaining security guards from Pilate. They personally accompanied the guards to the tomb and, as an added precaution, made sure that even a seal was set on the huge stone that enclosed the tomb (Mt. 27:62-66).

To say that perhaps Jesus never really died is absurd. He was executed by professional executioners. To revive from a near-death torture on Friday and make multiple appearances in various locales two days later with rapid moving from place to place would be impossible.

To say that Jesus' enemies stole the body is equally absurd. They would have displayed the stolen corpse to disprove the Resurrection.

The four basic pieces of evidence are: 1) the empty tomb with remnant body wrappings; 2) the breaking of the seal; 3) the moving of the massive stone; 4) the multiple presence of guards to prevent the stealing of the body.

To suppress the Christianity-caused upheaval in one of their conquered provinces, the Roman officials fought the proclamation of the Resurrection, even arresting Peter twice for preaching it. The Jewish leaders found their power, position, and religious beliefs threatened by Resurrection-bolstered Christianity. Efforts by both groups to suppress the Resurrection story failed because of evidence to the contrary.

The Resurrection of Jesus for us should have more than historical significance, or even a mere theological meaning. Spiritually, this climactic event took place "that, just as Christ was raised from the dead . . . we too may live a new life" (Rom. 6:4). Let us joyfully live it!

Did Jesus "rise from the dead" or was he raised from the dead?

There are about nineteen New Testament passages, chiefly in Paul's epistles, that clearly state that God the Father raised Jesus from the dead: for instance, 1 Thessalonians 1:10, 1 Corinthians 6:14; Galatians 1:1, etc. The Gospels, written after the epistles, use the Greek word, *egerthe*, that would normally be translated, "He was raised up." But in the Koine Greek used in the New Testament, this passive form can be translated with an active nuance: "He is risen" or "He rose" (See Mt. 28:6; Mk. 16:6; Lk. 24:6, 34). St. Jerome's latin translation was thus an active word: "surrexit" — "he has risen" — and this active form has been used in a number of Bible translations following Jerome's Vulgate. A more accurate and less controversial translation would be "He was raised." This would reflect the earliest Christology in the Church, pointing up Jesus' dependence on the Father in all things (Jn. 8:28-29).

Paul emphasizes the action of the Father in Jesus' resurrection to highlight the Father's "mighty strength which he exerted in Christ when he raised him from the dead" (Eph. 1:19-20). In at least ten places he says, "God the Father raised him from the dead." Only once (in 1 Thess. 4:14) he says that "Jesus . . . rose again" (as if by his own power); but such

83

limited phrase usage in no way tended to challenge Jesus' divinity.

However, John's later Christology was more refined. He emphasized that Jesus and the Father act by the very same divine power: "I and the Father are one" (Jn. 10:30). In that sense, it can be said that Jesus — "the resurrection and the life" (11:25) — rose by his own power: "I lay down my life — only to take it up again. . . . I have authority to lay it down and authority to take it up again. This command I received from my Father" (Jn. 10:17-18). Yet John uses the phrase "he was raised" (2:22), showing the option of designating either person as the power source of the Resurrection. "Whatever the Father does the Son also does. . . . Just as the Father raises the dead and gives them life, even so the Son gives life" (5:19:21). "All that belongs to the Father is mine" (16:15).

If "God raised [Jesus] from the dead" (Acts 2:24; see 2:32), then would not the Holy Spirit also be involved in the act of resurrection of Jesus? Indeed he was, for Jesus "was put to death . . . but made alive by the Spirit" (1 Pet. 3:18). Hence it was clearly the one Godhead in all three Persons of the Trinity that caused Jesus' resurrection.

Thus understood, there is no denial of Jesus dependence on the Father, no contradiction between rising and being raised, and no downgrading of emphasis on Jesus' own divinity.

Why does Jesus tell us to "be perfect" if only God is perfect?

The passage you quote (Mt. 5:48) is Jesus' summary of his teaching (vss. 43-48) about loving not just one's friends but also one's enemies, "that you may be children of [and thus resemble] your Father in heaven." The pericope, "Be perfect, as your heavenly Father is perfect" can be better understood in its parallel form in Luke 6:35-36: "The Most High . . . is kind to the ungrateful and wicked. Be merciful, just as your Father is merciful." Jesus simply says that God's perfection, manifested by his showing benevolent love indiscriminately to both good and evil persons, should be also our norm or goal.

The word "be" in the phrase "be perfect" in Matthew is in the future tense in the original Greek, thus indicating that this perfection is something to be striven for. In the corresponding passage in Luke, the "be" in "be merciful" is the present imperative tense, that is, a present command to do something in the future. Hence in both passages the word "be" implies a command to strive or become.

This mandate is obviously not a command to *attain* the infinite intrinsic perfection of God, but to resolve or *strive*, in our acts of mercy and kindness, to be "infinite" (that is limitless, without restricting our kindness to only good or friendly persons). The psalmist confronted this paradox of the limited and the limitless in the command for perfection: "To all perfection I see a limit; but your commands are limitless" (Ps. 119:96).

Since perfection in love, as the fulfillment of the law (Rom. 13:8-10), is perfection in holiness, it is only by perfection in love that we can "be holy as God is holy" (a concept cited four times in Leviticus and quoted in 1 Peter 1:16). This perfection in love requires that we never stop at what is merely obligatory or forced, but that we go further. Perfect human love, like God's love, is supererogatory.

"If someone takes your cloak, do not stop him from taking your tunic . . . and if anyone takes what belongs to you, do not demand it back. . . . Love your enemies, do good to them, and lend to them without expecting to get anything back. Then your reward will be great, and you will be children of the Most High, because he is kind to the ungrateful and wicked" (Lk. 6:29-35).

In Jesus' time in Palestine, Scripture was read by the rabbis in the synagogue in the original Hebrew, but the reading was often interpolated by a paraphrase (called a *targum*), which was spoken in Jesus' native language, Aramaic. As a commentary on Leviticus 22:26-28 (which prescribes kindness to animals), one of these oral *targums* ended with the words, "As our Father is merciful in heaven, so you must be merciful on earth." Jesus borrowed this phrase (Lk. 6:36), which was familiar to his hearers, and adapted it to impact the hearers with this challenge to imitate God's magnanimous love in dealing with others.

Mary

Must Catholics have a strong devotion to Mary?

Is it "necessary" to cultivate Marian devotion? The answer is No. Is such devotion in accordance with God's will and plan? The answer, based on Scripture, is Yes.

To question the "necessity" of Marian devotion is like suggesting that something need not be done at all if it can be done another way — somewhat like saying that since the Eucharist is not the *only* source of grace, we are free to neglect Communion. The point is that God has established a plan of sanctification, and we profit most when we recognize it and fulfill *all* of that plan.

Devotion to Mary or the saints, states Vatican II, involves not only depending on them for their intercession, as the Israelites did with Moses (see Ps. 106:23), or enjoying their fellowship in the "communion of saints" (i.e., believers in heaven and on earth: Eph. 3:15; Heb. 11:40; 12:1), but also imitating the good example of their life (Jas. 5:10). Marian devotion in this third form (imitating her virtues) will draw us closer to the Lord, whom she herself most closely resembles.

Paul presented himself for imitation in this way, as shown in seven passages inviting us to imitate him as reflecting Christ (1 Cor. 11:1; 4:16; 1 Thess. 1:6; Phil. 3:17, etc.). Paul's urging of others to imitate him was not an appeal to "distract" his spiritual clients from imitating Christ but to incite them to a closer imitation of Christ, for he wrote that the very meaning of Christian life is the imitation of Christ and the realization of his life in us (Eph. 5:1-2).

The rationale for Mary's preeminence in this patterning is that she did this better than anyone else; in her Christ's grace has been most truly realized. While Jesus is the perfect

Redeemer, Mary is the one most perfectly redeemed — the one in whom Christ's grace is most perfectly realized. By imitating her as the paradigm of all those redeemed, we become more like the Redeemer. The brilliance of the full moon is the reflection of the light of the sun, without which it would be totally dark. In the same way, Mary's virtue reflects God's own virtue. As the moon doesn't "distract" us from the sun but only reminds us of it, so does Mary remind us of God's goodness reflected in herself as God's most perfect creature. Admiring God's masterpiece is a compliment to the divine Artist. In Mary's own words, "The Mighty One has done great things for me — holy is *his* name" (Lk. 1:49).

To lack Marian devotion is to regard Mary as just another Christian, deserving of no greater veneration than anyone else. This would be a false and unscriptural position, in view of the triple reference to Mary in Chapter 1 of Luke's Gospel as "blessed" or most favored. Is it scriptural to refuse to relate to Mary in accordance with the Spirit-inspired word of God that "all generations will call me blessed" (Lk. 1:48)? With those sacred words in mind, it might be asked, why is it that only those with Marian devotion refer to her as the "*Blessed*" Virgin Mary?

If Jesus is the only mediator between God and humanity, isn't attention to Mary superfluous, or even distracting from a focus on Christ?

You are correct in stating that the Bible names Jesus as the only mediator between God and humans (1 Tim. 2:5; Acts 4:12; Heb. 7:25). However, in each of these citations, as the context shows, it refers to him as *redemptive* mediator (Savior or Redeemer). Mary's mediatorship is *non-redemptive*; it is only petitionary (impetrative) mediatorship, just as your own mediatorship would be if you prayed to God for me at my request. No Scripture passage states that Jesus is the only intercessor or *prayer* mediator — although he is the greatest one (Heb. 7:25, 9:24; Rom. 8:34; Is. 53:12; 1 Jn. 2:1), and the one through whom all prayer must *ultimately* pass to reach the Father (Jn. 14:6).

Vatican II states (*Lumen Gentium*, art. 62) that no creature, even Mary, can be put on the level of Jesus, the only Redeemer. However, just as Jesus' singular eternal priesthood is shared by both his ministers and the laity in various ways (I Pet. 2:5), and as his one goodness is radiated among creatures in various ways (1 Tim. 4:4), so also his unique mediation does not exclude but rather gives rise to a manifold shared mediation, in petitionary form, within which Mary's is preeminent.

It was this petitionary mediation that Paul requested of the Ephesians, asking them to pray "for all the saints [believers]" and he "prayed" for them to pray for himself (Eph. 6:18-19; 1 Thess. 5:25), while he himself prayed for others (Eph. 3:16; Col. 1:3), as did Epaphras (Col. 4:12). Mary's intercessory power with Jesus is of the same type as that of St. Paul and Epaphras, and the same as yours or mine, namely petitionary. But as the "highly favored one — full of grace" (Lk. 1:28), hers is far more powerful, as evidenced by her successful intercession for the embarrassed host at the Cana wedding, persuading Jesus to work his first miracle, even before his planned time (Jn. 2:4).

Mary in heaven is not deprived of that intercessory power that she exercised on earth, since heaven is a place not of deprivation but fulfillment, as implied in Hebrews 11:40. Even in the Old Testament we find examples of deceased persons (Jeremiah and Onias) prayerfully interceding for the living (2 Mac. 15:12-16). Those in heaven have more prayer power than they had on earth, for they are not faith-limited in heaven, since they see God directly (Job 19:26; 1 Cor. 13:12; 1 Jn. 3:2).

In response to your assertion that Marian devotion "distracts" from Christocentric devotion: Vatican II in the Constitution on the Church (art. 51) states, "Let the faithful be taught that our communion with those in heaven [by

89

veneration] . . . in no way diminishes the worship of adoration given to God the Father, through Christ, in the Spirit; on the contrary, it greatly enriches it." In the treatise on Mariology the same document states that Mary's salutary influence "flows from the merits of Christ, rests on his mediation . . . and draws all its power from it. *It does not hinder in any way the immediate union of the faithful with Christ, but on the contrary, fosters it* . . . it neither takes away nor adds anything to the dignity and efficacy of Christ, the one Mediator" (art. 60 and 62, quoting a formulation of St. Ambrose).

Your phrase, "praying to Mary," shows a misunderstanding common to both Catholics and non-Catholics, regarding Mary's role in our devotion. The Catholic Church does not teach us to pray *to* Mary or to any saint; if the phrase "pray to" is used in the strictest theological sense, it can be said that we pray only to God. But we do "prayerfully address" Mary, asking her to pray *for* us and *with* us to God, as in the Hail Mary: "pray *for* us sinners. . . "

Thus, Mary's mediation is not a "relay" system; she does not relay our needs to God as if they go through her to him. Rather, our prayers to God "parallel" her prayers to God for us, like two arrows going simultaneously Godward, in tandem. Mary doesn't stand "between" us and God to forward our prayers to him, but exercises her mediatorship by joining us in a fellowship of prayer, as mandated by Jesus: "If *two* of you agree to ask anything. . ." (Mt. 18:19).

Why is Mary so revered in Catholic teaching and tradition?

By bringing God to the human race, Mary became the model of the Church in that same function — a function for which it is called to be "without stain . . . holy and blameless" (Eph. 5:27). It was thus appropriate for God to predestine her to pattern his ideal for the Church, by keeping her immaculate and unstained.

To the serpent (Satan) in the Garden of Eden, after the "Fall," God said, "I will put *enmity between you and the woman*, and between your seed and her seed; he shall crush your head" (Gen 3:15). In this passage (called the "protoevangelium" or "prefigured Gospel") the word "he" refers to the woman's offspring, which in the Hebrew text is a masculine word, logically leading Christian tradition to refer to the woman's offspring as Christ; who else but Christ, by the redemption, would crush the head of the serpent? If this offspring of the woman is Christ, then the "woman" must be Mary, referred to prophetically, not Eve. The prophesied "enmity" between Satan and this woman, Mary, bespeaks an uncompromising opposition between the initiator of *sin* and a *sinless* woman, who was most highly graced or "full of grace" as totally sinless.

Mary, as the God-assigned "enemy" of Satan, would have to be one who had never been under his dominion by either original or personal sin, in order to be maximally worthy to tabernacle in her body the "Offspring" prophesied in Genesis — the sinless God Incarnate — and bring him forth to redeem a sin-filled world.

The prophesied victory of "crushing" the power of Satan would not be a meaningful victory if the conquering Redeemer had assumed his body from a woman who had been subject to the Adversary (which is the very meaning of "Satan"). Christ's victory would have been only a Pyrrhic victory if his suffering and glorified Body — the very instrument of the victorious redemption (1 Cor. 11:24) — had been drawn from a mother who had been contaminated or "conquered" by his enemy through sin. Christ would not derive his sinless body from a mother's body that had been even slightly sin-contaminated.

These are a few of the multifarious insights that the Spirit has delivered to the Church in the gradual Scripture-based development of Mariology through the centuries. The theological insights mentioned here deal with only one Marian privilege — her Immaculate Conception.

Let us never weary of praising God, as Mary did, for all she has received from him for *us* to enjoy and admire. Truly, "he who is mighty has done great things" for us by doing such great things for Mary, as "our tainted nature's solitary boast." As part of "all generations" that will call her blessed, let us admire and honor God's splendiferous masterpiece; in doing so we will be implicitly honoring the divine Artist himself who fashioned her.

Why does the Church teach that Mary was immaculately conceived when the Bible says that all have sinned but Christ?

First of all, the Immaculate Conception does *not* refer to the miraculous conception of Jesus in the womb of Mary — the virgin birth; it refers rather to her exemption from original sin from the time of her own conception in the womb of St. Ann. And, by extension, it also refers to her preservation from personal sin throughout her life.

There is no doubt that Mary was redeemed or "saved"; yet she was conceived without sin, or immaculate. The solution to this paradox was first formulated by the medieval Franciscan theologian Duns Scotus — a solution eventually incorporated into the 1854 proclamation of the dogma of the Immaculate Conception. (This proclamation was not a reaction to heresy, but a declaration of a long-held truth finally *defined after having been refined* theologically through the centuries.)

Scotus pointed out that just as health can come either by way of *prevention of disease* or by way of *cure of disease*, so can salvation — the reception of redemption. *Mary was "saved"* or redeemed *before* Jesus' redemptive act, by the *anticipatory application of that redemptive act* (in God there is no sequence of time). "*In view of the foreseen merits of Jesus Christ" (not by her own merits),* says the document, Mary was *prevented* from inheriting original sin from the moment of her conception; also, by the same Christ-earned merits, she was preserved free of any personal sin during her entire life. By her pre-Calvary redemption, it was as if she were "given merchandise before the check was cashed," so to speak.

This "preservative redemption" was basically the *perfect* redemption, since it involved not the healing of sin but the preventing of sin. This "perfect redemption" inspired the poet Wordsworth to forthrightly acclaim Mary as "Our tainted nature's solitary boast."

Regarding the biblical statement of Romans 3:23, that "*all* have sinned," two things must be kept in mind: first, the word "all," if taken with absolute literalness, would have to include Christ, which is absurd (see Heb. 4:15); and second, the context of Romans 3:23 (as every reference to the universality of sin) shows an emphasis on the truth that *all* human beings need redemption (see verse 24). Jesus — the only one who *by his very nature* was sinless, and hence the only one who could redeem us — didn't need redemption, of course. Mary *is included* among all those needing redemption, even though for her it was "preventive" rather than "curative."

Unlike Jesus, *"Mary was not sinless by her own nature,"* wrote Pope Pius IX; only by God's grace was she immaculate (unstained by sin). And Mary knew that only God could "create a clean heart" (Ps. 51:10), so she didn't hesitate to acknowledge God as the source of her gifts: "He who is mighty has done great things for me" (Lk. 1:49).

Personal Morality

Do we really have free will?

Yes, through grace God entices the human will to respond to his promptings, but without impugning the freedom of that will in any way. Romans 9 is largely devoted to considering how that sovereign grace relates to the elect (chosen for salvation) and the non-elect (those not thus chosen). Paul gives the example of the twins, Jacob, chosen by God, and Esau, rejected by God even before birth (vs. 13), to show that "election" or predestination is not wholly determined by one's works (vs. 12).

There cannot be moral goodness without the possibility of moral evil. Freedom to choose good necessarily implies freedom to choose evil — with the terrible consequences that ensue from that choice. But man is totally and ultimately responsible for his own sin, and God bears no responsibility for it in any degree whatever. In view of Acts 17:30, stating that God "commands *all* people everywhere to repent," there is implied a standing offer of forgiveness. This in turn implies that God doesn't force anyone to commit evil or remain in the state of sin. No one is "beyond recovery" (Rom. 11:11).

Addressing the issue of unbelieving Jews, Paul says, "Consider the kindness and the sternness of God; sternness to those who fell, but kindness to you, *provided* that you continue in his kindness. And *if* they do not persist in unbelief, they will be grafted in [the olive root]" (Rom. 11:22-23). These words of condition, "*provided*" and "*if*," imply that God has not paralyzed the freedom of the will in his sanctions.

To sum up, then, God chooses from all eternity those who will be saved, based on his sovereign good pleasure. Yet "whoever refuses to believe will be condemned" (Mk. 16:16).

The God who does not want "anyone to perish, but everyone to come to repentance" (2 Pet. 3:9) will not make the choice for them. Each person bears the full responsibility for his own choice. He must decide for himself between life and death, between blessings and curses (Deut. 30:19). God's predestinative choice is contingent on our free choice foreknown infallibly by him. Thus his sovereignty and our free will are both left intact.

Does the Bible forbid abortion as a crime?

It is very definitely indicated in Psalm 139:13 that God's personal regard for the embryo begins from the time of conception, when it is referred to as a person: "You formed my inward parts, you knit me together in my mother's womb." ("Me" indicates personhood, not just an organism.) If it is a *person* that is killed by abortion, then abortion is murder.

The Psalmist continues (vs. 16): "Your eyes saw my unformed substance; all the days ordained for me were written in your book before one of them came to be." Thus abortion not only aborts the child, but also it aborts the ordained plans of God for that child.

The modern science of biogenetics affirms that all genetic features to be later developed in the adult are already present in the fecundated ovum from the very beginning: "I praise you because I am fearfully and wonderfully made; your works are wonderful. . ." (vs. 14). Ecclesiastes 11:5 reminds us, "As you do not know how the spirit comes to the bones in the womb of a woman with child, so you do not know the work of God who makes everything," including the unborn child. Destroying a human life made to the image and likeness of God is a very serious matter, not something like killing a cockroach.

In Jeremiah 1:5 the Lord says to the prophet, "Before I formed you in the womb I knew you; before you were born I consecrated you." Thus it is seen that we humans have an

identity in the mind of God that is "from everlasting" —
obviously prior to conception by those natural processes that
bring about the miracle of human life (see Job 31:15). Beyond
that fact, the Jeremiah passage emphasizes the staggering truth
that God has a definite plan and purpose for our lives, and that
each of us really matters to him. Consequently, anyone who
takes a human life at any stage will have to reckon with God. In
Genesis 9:5 God tells Noah, "From each man I will demand an
accounting for the life of his fellowman." Abortionists and
women planning abortions should consider this interdiction
seriously.

In Isaiah 49:1 the prophet says, "The Lord called me before
my birth. From within the womb he called me by my name."
Like Jeremiah, Isaiah was called before birth, as was the
Apostle Paul, from his mother's womb (Gal. 1:15). All this
makes it obvious that personhood is present before birth, and
taking the life of a person is homicide (apart from cases where
the right to life is forfeited, as in cases of crimes deserving of
capital punishment, and cases of self-defense — including
national self-defense in war).

It is interesting to speculate how the U.S. Supreme Court
would answer the question, at what point in the gestation period
of Christ in Mary's womb was the "Word made flesh" as a
human? Or, to speak the unspeakable, if Mary had an abortion,
beyond what point of her pregnancy would that have meant the
death of Christ? After one month? After one day? After one
minute? Or to rephrase the question, when did the miracle of
the Incarnation take place? Was it not at the very moment of
conception? A serious consideration of this major biblical event
would put the abortion issue in perspective.

John the Baptist before birth (Lk. 1:41) manifested the
fulfillment of the prophecy of the angel to Zechariah (vs. 15)
that he (John) would be "filled with the Holy Spirit even from
his mother's womb." This occurred when he was six months
into gestation (vs. 36). The Holy Spirit doesn't fill a "blob of

tissue," but a human being. Hence, if this human being had been aborted at that time, clearly it would have been murder.

In biblical times, incest reaped the death penalty (Lev. 20:11, 12, 14, 17, etc.) for the perpetrators, but not for the child that might be conceived from the incestuous relationship, thus supporting the protection of innocent human life, no matter how sinful the act that brought that life into being. Thus the Bible has something to say to those who tolerate abortion only in cases of incest or rape. Abortion in any case is still murder.

Other biblical passages that indicate personhood from the time of conception include Psalm 51:5. "I was born a sinner, yes, from the moment my mother conceived me." This statement about original sin inherited from our protoparents Adam and Eve would not have any meaning if the embryo were not human from the moment of conception.

In early biblical times, the closest thing to abortion was infanticide at the time of birth, as when the Pharaoh commanded the Hebrew midwives to kill all male Hebrew children at birth (Ex. 1:16). God punished this baby-killing by sending "defiling floods" on the land (Wis. 11:7).

Ultimately, the whole abortion issue, in biblical terms, is summed up by the words of God through Moses in Deuteronomy 30:19: "I have set before you life and death, blessings and curses. Now *choose life*, so that you and your children may live."

Is abortion really murder?

Yes, direct abortion (not miscarriage or stillbirth) is murder.

Today in the United States one pregnancy out of every four ends in surgical abortion. But surgical abortion was not technically possible in biblical times. Unborn babies were killed only when the mother was slain also, as in Amos 1:13, where it is recorded that Ammon "ripped open the pregnant woman of Gilead" (as a form of brutal genocide that God

97

punished by a tumult of nature and deprivation of national leadership).

In cases of rape or incest, there is no doubt that the woman is usually a victim of injustice. But this does not give her the right to perpetrate a further injustice on the child in her womb by killing it. (Adopting the child out to couples eager for a child is usually the best solution in cases where the mother doesn't really want the child. This is especially true in cases of incest, where a relative fathered the child, who might discover the fact later.)

Pre-birth infanticide (abortion) is no less serious than postnatal killing. Thus, when an abortion attempt fails and the fetus is still alive, the doctor by law must try to preserve the same life he had tried to kill only moments before. The absurdity of this situation is that the fetus was regarded as a non-person during the abortion attempt, but as a person when the abortion failed. Within moments, the premature but living fetus "acquired personhood," according to the law, by simply being removed from the uterus! How could pro-abortion advocates explain this absurdity? Obviously, it must be deduced that abortion is infanticide — clearly murder, explicitly forbidden by God's commandment (Ex. 20:13; Deut. 5:17; Mt. 5:21).

The pro-choice stance that "a woman has a right to her own body" is contrary to Scripture, since Paul says that we do not own our bodies (1 Cor. 6:19); we are merely stewards of these temples of the Holy Spirit, and must not abuse them, or the bodies of others, including unborn children, who are a "heritage from the Lord" (Ps. 127:3).

Prayer

Doesn't Scripture say that we shouldn't pray for those in serious sin?

Like Jesus, who "made intercession for transgressors" (Is. 53:12), we too should pray for *all* sinners, even the worst, for "whoever turns a sinner away from his error will save him from [eternal] death and cover many sins" (James 5:20). We are urged to "snatch others from the fire and save them" (Jude 23). Paul certainly prayed for sinners needing salvation: "My heart's desire and *prayer* to God . . . is that they may be saved" (Rom. 10:1).

The scriptural passage that you refer to about not praying for some sinners is found in I John 5:16-17. This enigmatic passage is open to at least six interpretations, but none that might contradict the above statements from the Bible. Let me quote that passage in full, from the New American Bible translation:

"Anyone who sees his brother sinning, if the sin is not deadly, should petition God, and thus life will be given to the sinner. This is only for those whose sin is not deadly. There is such a thing as a deadly sin; I do not say that one should pray about that. True, all wrongdoing is sin, but not all sin is deadly."

The two verses just before the one quoted state that we can know that God hears us if we ask anything in accordance with his will, this passage at first tells us of the kind of petition we can be sure God will answer. Yet, in the context of this epistle directed against Gnostic teaching, which denied Jesus' incarnation and disregarded all moral restraints, it is probable that the "deadly sin" or "sin that leads to death" refers to the Gnostics' adamant and persistent denial of the truth and to their shameless and *unrepentant* immorality. Such unrepented sin leads to spiritual death, and hence is "deadly" (Eph. 2:1: "You were dead in your transgressions").

While it is commendable to petition God to overlook a person's faults or venial sins, one could not ask that same petition for one living in the horrendous state of mortal or "deadly" sin, since such a person is living in a state of total rejection of God and his will. God cannot overlook the evil of anyone who maliciously and deliberately continues to reject him as the very Deity on whom he depends for both physical and spiritual life. A person with only venial sin is still on a road headed Godward, but is off on a rough shoulder or in a ditch. A person living in mortal sin is on the same road but going the wrong direction, away from God, and needs to make a "U-turn" (a metanoia or radical change of direction) to be directed toward God, his Creator, as his ultimate destiny.

To remove such a serious sin would require a sincere act of repentance or contrition on the part of the sinner. This act of contrition (that is, the *prayer of repentance*) could not be made vicariously by another person. Yet for a person with only failings or venial sins, a *prayer of petition* (could be made by another, asking God in his mercy to overlook or discount such failings, as Moses prayed for the Israelites in their fickleness (Ex. 32:12).

Is there any kind of prayer that can be said for a person living in serious sin? Yes. Anyone can and should pray that God gives the sinner an actual grace to repent, and thus receive God's forgiveness. Of course, this grace can be rejected by the free will of the sinner, which is never forced by God — for then the will wouldn't be free. Such a prayer for a sinner is not a repentance prayer to substitute for the sinner's personal repentance prayer; it is a prayer that the sinner be motivated to freely decide to pray a repentance prayer.

Persistent rejection of such graces or "promptings of the Holy Spirit" can lead to the sin against the Holy Spirit, with a consequent "hardening of the heart," as happened to the Pharaoh who obstinately withstood God's demands given through Moses (Ex. 14:8). The sin against the Holy Spirit is called the "unforgivable sin" (Mt. 12:32; Lk. 12:10; Mk. 3:29). In its various forms it is ultimately a rejection of forgiveness offered by the dispenser of divine forgiveness, the Holy Spirit. *It is unforgivable, not because God refuses to forgive, but because the sinner refuses to be forgiven*, maliciously but freely choosing to remain in spiritual death, which could be reversed by a simple apology to God. While such a person chooses to remain unrepentant, others' prayers for him remain unavailing. It would be like trying to push a car whose driver insists on keeping his foot on the brake. It is useless to ask God in prayer to give such a person the divine life of *sanctifying grace*, but we can always ask God to flood him with *actual grace* that might entice him to repent (without impugning his free will, of course).

There are several other interpretations of this difficult passage from the first epistle of John, but the one I have presented here is the most theologically acceptable one. With the above distinctions in mind, we can see why John writes, "I do not say that one should pray about that" (deadly sin). In effect, he is saying that intercessory prayer for persons in mortal sin is useless *if* it is either substitutionary repentance prayer or prayer for God to give them the life of grace while they refuse to accept it.

Is it valid to pray for the intercession or help of a guardian angel?

To cultivate devotion to your guardian angel, I suggest that you meditate on the personalism entailed in that classic pericope from Psalm 91:11 (and the surrounding passages): "He will command his angels concerning *you* to guard *you* in all *your* ways." This reflects God's personal interest in *you* as an individual, in sending you such a "customized" gift.

It would be unthinkable to culpably ignore or neglect such

an awesome personal and personalized gift from God, given to guard you "in all your ways" — in your ups and downs, in your waking and sleeping hours, when you're alone or with others, in your joys and in your sufferings, in your successes and your failures. "Make yourself familiar with angels," urges St. Frances de Sales, "and behold them frequently in spirit; for without being seen, they are present with you."

Your appreciation of your guardian angel will reach its scintillating climax at your death, when he takes you by the hand to lead you to the arms of God, while, as Shakespeare phrased it, "flights of angels sing thee to thy rest." And as your close personal friend, who has known you better than anyone, your angel will rejoice along with you for all eternity in the ineffable bliss of the vision of God.

Truly, those who believe this doctrine of guardian angels with all their hearts are utterly transformed in time and for all eternity!

How can I find out what is the best method of prayer for my own life?

Don't feel that you must imitate every saint or even any one saint in every respect. Rather, look upon them as reminders that each human being is called in a *unique way* to holiness; each of us is asked to become attentive to God's voice in our own unique lives as individuals. His sheep know his voice (Jn. 10:4), but the call is individual and unique to each sheep, since "he calls his own sheep by name and leads them out" (vs. 3). One person is close to God in a garden, another in a chapel, another is rhapsodized by music, another surrounded by bubbly children; another encounters God in the awesome study of astronomy and the wonders of the universe or in the fascinating beauties and marvels of the undersea world. Some can worship God by free-flowing liturgical dance, others by singing hymns or psalms, some by Spirit-filled reading of God's word (Col.

3:16). The modalities of God-encounter are endless. Once the basic mandated means are fulfilled, such as the reception of the sacraments, familiarity with God's word, etc.; try to expand your sensitivity to as many grace avenues as possible, but let "the Spirit breathe where he will" (Jn. 3:8) in his sovereign choice as to *how* you are meant to grow holy. In this way, every facet of your life will become a kind of communing with God, and your union with him will grow more intimate and more fulfilling as you mature in the Spirit. At that point you'll be fulfilling Paul's injunction to "pray continually" (1 Thess. 5:17).

How can I pray better?

Even a lengthy retreat wouldn't be enough to give a really adequate answer to your question. But perhaps a few principles may be of help to you.

First of all, remember that prayer is not talking *to* God but talking *with* God. That means you must learn to listen as well as speak (Ps. 46:10). God spoke to Peter, who was chattering at the transfiguration scene: "This is my beloved Son. *Listen* to him" (Mk. 9:7). We should be, especially in prayer, "quick to listen, slow to speak" (Jas. 1:19).

Second, although petition is good ("Ask and you shall receive"), still we should not let our petitions eclipse our praise, worship, adoration and thanksgiving prayer (Col. 3:17), but accompany our petitions with worship and gratitude (Phil. 4:6).

Keep in mind that "the Lord is near" (vs. 5), so that prayer is not a long-distance phone call to heaven, but a casual and intimate conversation with a Friend close at hand, even abiding with each one who loves him (Jn. 14:23), revealing himself to such a person (vs. 21).

Third, try to see how, in the context of your ordinary life, God is teaching you and conversing with you; it might be through a sunset, a child's tear, the wag of your dog's tail, or the comfort of a soft pillow, as well as your headache, your fears (nudging you in a "fear-not" invitation to trust), or your financial problems reminding you to "seek first the kingdom of God, and all these things will be given besides" (Mt. 6:33). You don't need to go beyond your normal experience to encounter God, although you should broaden that experience to include the sacraments, especially the Eucharist, the community forms of prayer, such as the liturgy or prayer meetings (Heb. 10:25), and the rosary (which is really more of a mental prayer than a vocal prayer, since the Our Fathers and Hail Marys in decade form are Scripture words that provide a time measurement of meditating on the Scripture-based "mysteries" of the rosary). St. Paul also encourages prayer in the Spirit (praying in tongues) as a special way of praying that assures us we are praying in accordance with God's will (Rom, 8:26-27).

Fourth, don't tie yourself to one form of prayer only. Paul says in Ephesians 6:18: "Pray in the Spirit [as the Spirit leads] on all occasions, with *all kinds* of prayers and requests." It's not important whether you use books or not, as St. Francis of Assisi told his friars. There should be confidence and self-surrender in your prayer, but also a concern for others who need your prayers of intercession.

Fifth, regarding mental prayer, whether the more active form called meditation, or a more passive form called contemplation, the advice of the modern mystic Evelyn Underhill is always appropriate: "The type of prayer best for you is that to which you feel drawn in your best and quietest times, and in which it is easiest for you to remain aware of God's presence and love." An extremely high form of prayer is often neglected because it is absurdly simple; it consists of simply "basking in the sunshine of God's love" — wordlessly. This prayer is most delightful to the Heart of God, and draws down so many graces and blessings that petition often seems superfluous.

Why is there a difference between the Protestant "Our Father" and the Catholic version of the prayer?

Almost the only translation of the Bible that includes the added words in the text of the Our Father (Mt. 6:13) is the King James version, used mostly by Protestants. The added words are: "For thine is the kingdom, and the power, and the glory, forever. Amen." This closing phrase was not used by Jesus when he taught the Lord's Prayer, but was written in later Bible manuscripts as a "gloss" (marginal addition made by a copyist when Bibles were hand-written). It is an ancient liturgical prayer that has four components: kingdom, power (might), glory, and eternity. These elements are often woven together in Scripture passages such as 1 Chronicles 29:10-11, Psalm 1455:11-12 and 24:8, and Rev. 5:12. When the Lord's Prayer is recited or sung during the Mass, this enclitic ending is separated from the original Lord's prayer by an "embolism" prayer, to emphasize that it is not part of the original Lord's Prayer but worthy of retaining as a beautiful and ancient Scripture-based prayer used in Eastern and Western liturgies.

This closing doxology is not found in the earliest biblical manuscripts (neither the Matthew 6 or the Luke 11 quoting of the Lord's Prayer), nor is it recorded in the early Church Fathers' commentaries. Yet as a liturgical addition it lends a smoother ending to the Lord's Prayer, and provides an appropriate climax to the several classical musical renditions of that great prayer. Moreover, it is a strong counterpoint to the last phrase, "deliver us from the evil one," since it points up the ascendancy of the kingdom of God over the kingdom of the devil.

How can saints, as dead persons, intercede for us, the living?

If I pray for my own growth in holiness and ask you to pray for that same intention for me, our prayers become like two parallel arrows moving Godward; it is not a relay system, with one arrow pushing the other to God. Thus, you don't get "between" me and God as you pray for me. Likewise, the angels and saints whom I ask to pray for me, don't get between me and God to relay my prayers to him. They simply join their prayers to mine; it's "two agreeing to ask something" in Jesus' name (Mt. 18:19-20). In fact, they may "intercede" for me even when I don't pray at all, since they are "fellow citizens with God's people and members of God's household" (Eph. 2:19), but are joined with me in Jesus (verse 10), who is the ultimate mediator before the Father. They are a part of the "communion of saints" (believers) in the great prayer fellowship, part of the Father's "whole family of believers in heaven and on earth" (Eph. 3:15). Vatican II reminds us that the early Christians asked the intercession of the apostles after their death.

As I can ask you to pray for me — and I do — I also ask God's blessed saints to pray for me. Thus I pray not really to them, but with them, and they with me, for my needs.

Why did Jesus teach us to pray "lead us not into temptation" when Scripture says that God tempts no one?

All temptations come ultimately from any of three sources — the world, the devil, or the flesh — but not from God. In both passages that you refer to — the Our Father and James's statement (1:13) — the Greek word "*peirasmos*" is used (or its derivative). My Greek dictionary says that the primary meaning is trial or a putting to proof; solicitation, provocation, or testing. However, by implication it can also mean adversity or temptation. It seems that James is using the word in its extended meaning of temptation, while Jesus' use of the word was put into the Greek in its primary meaning of trial or adversity. The original word that Jesus used in his native language (Aramaic) is lost, but the Greek and Latin translations derived from it do not convey primarily the idea of solicitation to commit sin, as the English word "temptation" implies. In the passage from James, the secondary meaning is intended, as the context shows, while Jesus, it seems, intended the primary meaning in the Our Father.

In the Our Father, the word is meant to convey the idea of testing, or proving, as God "tempted" Abraham (Gen. 22:1) — the Hebrew word "*nacah*" — to test, although it is translated "tempt." Hence, probably more correctly, the Lord's Prayer in the Jerusalem Bible reads: "Do not put us to the test," and the New American Bible reads: "subject us not to the trial."

This trial or testing may well be that which Jesus spoke of in Luke 21:36: "Pray always that you may be accounted worthy to escape all these things that shall come to pass" (the horrors of the great trial or tribulation at the end times). This end-time tribulation which Jesus refers to extensively in the synoptic Gospels may well be the trial or tribulation referred to in Daniel 12:1, which also refers to God's people being delivered from evil, thus linking the last two phrases of the Lord's prayer in that prophetic utterance (see also Joel 2:2). Certainly God does not lead us into temptation, just as a lawmaker does not tempt a criminal to break the law; however, he may providently engineer trials for us, as he did for Abraham, Job, Jonah, etc. And those trials could also be sent as a purifying punishment from his hand for a rebellious mankind. Jesus' Gethsemane prayer restates the Lord's prayer; thus, "Watch and pray that you do not undergo the test" is more appropriate than "Do not enter into temptation."

Let us suppose that "temptation" is the correct translation for the Lord's prayer. Then we may follow the interpretation of second-century luminaries like St. Cyril: "Do not let us be led into temptation," or "Do not let us be tempted beyond our strength" — referring to Paul's remark in 1 Cor. 10:13. But I personally agree with the majority of theologians who accept the translation "Subject us not to the trial" — that is, the great tribulation at the end times. This better parallels Jesus' prophecies about that time of trial that he asks us to pray to escape in Luke 21:36.

Relationships and Roles

Doesn't St. Paul's direction that women "be silent" in church prohibit the modern ministry of women as lectors, teachers, prayer leaders, and the like?

The two references of Paul prohibiting women from speaking in church are 1 Cor. 14:34-35 and 1 Tim. 2:11. There are five explanations of these passages that should be understood before blatantly labeling Paul as anti-feminist, as many ill-informed Bible readers do today.

1) Some scripture scholars doubt that the first passage was even written by Paul; it may be a "gloss" inserted by a scribe in a later redaction.

2) Even if Paul did author that passage, just as in 1 Cor. 11, he is not dealing here with male-female relations in general, but with propriety in worship, based on acculturated behavior patterns of his day in that part of the world. As Pope John Paul II pointed out, uncompromising doctrinal matters in Scripture must be distinguished from norms that have only cultural significance for a limited time and place.

3) Husbands and wives are to be in submission *to each other* (Eph. 5:21), though in different ways — the wife through reverential obedience, and the husband through Christlike self-sacrificing love to please his wife (vss. 22-28). This double submission was to be manifest not just in the home, but also in public worship. The wife's respectful submission to her husband — *not to other men* — was to be manifest by her reserved and quiet demeanor in public, since the local custom among the Corinthians regarded it as disgraceful for a woman to speak out in open inquiry in church rather than manifesting the wifely type of submission by asking her husband privately

(1 Cor. 14:35); she was not to embarrass him in such a violation of the local norms of public decorum.

4) The phrase, "be silent" is a faulty translation of the Greek word *sigatosan* (verse 34), which can better be translated as "hold their peace," since the previous sentence reminds them that the Lord who is worshiped in that assembly is a God of peace, not confusion. It was *disorderly* speaking that was prohibited, such as unruly chattering among the Corinthian women that often followed a prophecy or message given in tongues with its interpretation. This more proper translation also avoids an apparent contradiction, because in the same epistle Paul implies that *women are free to speak in church* by way of public prayer, giving prophecies and tongue-speaking (14:39-40 and 11:5).

5) Paul forbids women to teach (1 Tim. 2:12), but the context shows that women are forbidden only to teach their husbands if it is done *arrogantly*, "usurping the authority of the man" (verse 12), or perhaps usurping the authority of the male overseers (bishops) (3:2). Some women, like those at Ephesus, were man-domineering and poorly instructed, so Paul insisted on their submissive *learning* (verse 11) before attempting to teach. Paul insists on orderly and mutual (but different) spouse submission, not subjugation, and certainly not spouse inequality.

What does the New Testament say about the roles of husband and wife?

In husband-wife relationships, the New Testament clearly declares the equal-but-different status of spouses who must "submit to each other" (Eph. 5:21) — the wife by reverential obedience, and the husband by self-sacrificing love (see also 1 Pet. 3:1-8). Commenting on the Ephesian passage in August, 1982, Pope John Paul II said:

"Paul did not mean that the husband is the 'boss' of the wife, not that matrimony is a pact of dominion of a husband over wife; there is to be no one-sided domination. Each is to be subject to the other from a sense of Christian piety that finds expression in love. Our contemporary awareness is certainly different from that of Paul's time, as is the mentality, customs, and social position of women in relation to men. Nevertheless, the fundamental principles we find in the letter to the Ephesians remain the same."

What are those principles? There are four of them to be kept in mind in the emotion-charged atmosphere of the issue of feminism: 1) the principle of *order*. Because of the order of creation, with Adam having been created before Eve (1 Tim. 2:13; 1 Cor. 11:9), there is to be an ordinating by subordinating (not subjugating) wife to husband by reason of authority, not dignity. This wifely subordination (Eph. 5:22) differs from that of a child relating to a parent (6:4).

2) The principle of *mutual submission*, obediential on the wife's part (vs. 22), and self-sacrificial on the husband's part (vs. 25). Both domineering men and power-grabbing women "libbers" are far from the submissive spirit of Jesus, "who, being in the very nature of God, did not consider equality with God something to be grasped, but took the nature of a servant" (Phil. 2:6-7). The mutual spousal submission is one of the five signs associated with being Spirit-filled (Eph. 5:18-22). "Honor one another above yourselves," Paul urges (Rom. 12:10).

3) The principle of *freedom* associated with human dignity, in which the "Spirit blows freely" with his free gifts to be used freely by both men and women (Rom. 12:6). Certainly freedom has "fences"; if one were to exercise his freedom to drive on the wrong side of the street, his freedom would be curtailed by a jail, hospital, or morgue. The Church leaders are God-empowered to decide where the freedom "fences" are (1 Thess. 5:12; Heb. 5:12), based on biblical reasons.

4) The principle of *love*, which should pervade every aspect of Christian family and married life and all dialogue (Rom. 12:9-16; Col. 3:14). The women's-rights issue is surely a

sensitive one, but anyone can agree to disagree in love without patronizing or matronizing.

Pope John Paul II called the women's liberation movement a "movement of the Spirit" for our time — but only when it extols women's rights and dignity without advocating an anti-biblical stance or immorality (James 1:21), such as lesbianism, abortion, prostitution, fornication, cohabitation without marriage, etc. Free of such moral pollution, "women's lib" is a breath of fresh air needed for our modern society — truly a manifestation of the "Breath of God" that is the Holy Spirit himself.

As a Christian, how can I help a person who is very negative and difficult?

A negative person is one who is embittered by a series of circumstances from the past — perhaps some injustice done to one, or a prolonged love-deprivation, especially from parents. It's hard for such a person to dwell on the good and pleasant things, as Paul advises the Philippians (4:8), so bitterness envelops the negative individual like quicksand. The person becomes sort of rooted in a kind of conscious or subconscious hostility that leads to further problems; as it says in Heb. 12:15, "Watch out that no bitterness takes root . . . for as it springs up it causes deep trouble, hurting many in their spiritual lives." Many such persons can't lift themselves from that quicksand of negativity and may resist any help offered. Indirectly, however, you can help such a person in five ways:

First, listen attentively; that's difficult, but negative persons seldom get listened to in a caring way.

Second, don't let the person bring out the worst in you, for such a one can contaminate your own emotions, pulling you into a negative frame of mind, making you angry, uncooperative, etc. Ignore a bitter remark, or change the

111

subject, or counter with a positive remark calmly. Proverbs 15:1 is still true: "A soft answer turns away wrath."

Third, state the facts simply to correct the person's distorted view of a situation. Don't use a "see-how-wrong-you-are" attitude, but exercise consummate patience in presenting the situation objectively. Prayerfully study James 3:16-18.

Fourth, direct some attention to practical problem solving. Occasionally such bitter persons have legitimate complaints. Remind the person that there are always some things that can be changed, if only our attitudes (Col. 3:12-15).

Fifth, make the situation a continuing matter of prayer; this is the most important rule for dealing with negativity. Before praying for a change of that person's attitudes, we must pray for our own attitudes with humility, then the Lord will often change us and work through us to change the negative person to think more positively.

Perhaps the best way to help a negative person is to keep from becoming negative ourselves about their problem, and then to pour on the love. This is one of the most challenging forms of Christian charity, perhaps one that Paul had in mind when he wrote the masterful treatise on love in 1 Cor. 13.

Sacraments and Sacred Things

How does the sacrament of confirmation relate to the "baptism in the Holy Spirit"?

Though baptism and confirmation were typically conferred together in the early Church, that practice changed. Under the influence of Peter Lombard, the great eleventh-century sacramentologist, the anointing of confirmation became isolated from baptism as a separate sacrament, reserved to the bishop so as to dignify the sacrament with the splendor of a liturgical ceremony. It thus enhanced the sacrament externally (liturgically) but it lost two elements by a kind social attrition. It was no longer "ecclesial" (congregational) but "ecclesiastical" (hierarchically administered); and secondly, there was soon lost all *expectancy* of the outpouring of the charismatic gifts, especially tongues, as mentioned (directly or indirectly) in all of the New Testament baptism-in-the-Spirit experiences.

It is thus obvious why the baptism in the Spirit and charismatic gifts are not usually received at confirmation services today, as should be expected, ideally. The candidates are usually taught to seek *only* the seven personal gifts of the Holy Spirit listed in Isaiah 11:2. Grace, but not usually the baptism in the Spirit, is received today at confirmation. Hence the reason for encouraging people to make a "Life in the Spirit Seminar" to "complete" their confirmation graces.

What is the difference between the sacraments of

baptism and confirmation, both of which are said to confer the Holy Spirit?

What we call confirmation is a post-baptism Spirit-life — the "promise of the Father," as Jesus called it (Acts 1:4). It was the Pentecost experience, a follow-up of water baptism (vs. 5). At Pentecost itself, Peter urged all to receive both baptisms (of water and Spirit) in sequence (2:38). Paul actually did this: After rebaptizing the twelve John-baptized Ephesians, he led them into the baptism in the Spirit: "When Paul placed his hands on them, the Spirit came on them, and they spoke in tongues and prophesied" (19:6).

How does the baptism with water relate to the baptism in the Spirit? We certainly receive the Holy Spirit when we are baptized in water. But this presence, as St. Thomas Aquinas says, is that of the *indwelling* (*inhabitatio*) of the Holy Spirit, not the *infilling* (*infusio*) of the Holy Spirit, which is the baptism in the Spirit — the Pentecostal experience. This is a distinction Jesus made in John 14:17, using the words "with you" vs. "within you" — a distinction implied by Paul's remark in Romans 8:9 about the controlling power of the Spirit when he is *within* us. (i.e., when we are baptized in the Holy Spirit).

How does the sacrament of confirmation fit into all this? The sacrament of confirmation by the laying on of hands after water baptism, while invoking the Holy Spirit (as in Acts 19:6), was formalized in the early Church as a sacramental act designed to induce the baptism in the Spirit. It was usually subsequent to water baptism, but not always — as in the case of Cornelius (Acts 10:44-48) and that of Paul himself (Acts 9:17-18). Paul was probably referring to this sacrament, later called confirmation, when in Ephesians 4:30 he says, "Do not grieve the Holy Spirit of God, with whom you were *sealed* for the day of redemption."

How did the baptism given by John the Baptist differ from the baptism given after the death of Jesus?

John's baptism is referred to in all four Gospels: Matthew 3:11; Mark 1:4; Luke 3:16; John 1:26 and 33. His baptizing of repentant persons was so characteristic of his ministry that he became known as John the Baptist or Baptizer. He did this in the "desert region" (Mk. 1:4) just west of the Dead Sea, where the Essenes, one sect of pre-Christian Jews, practiced a ritual baptism (baptismal pits are still extant there near where the Dead Sea scrolls were found). His baptismal ritual was simply a water baptism that was preceded or accompanied by repentance. John's audience had known of baptism for Gentile converts to Judaism, but had not heard that Jews needed to repent and be baptized (see Mt. 3:9-11).

Submitting to a ritual "washing" was recognized as an external act of professing of the *need to be cleansed* from sin, but, reminiscent of the earlier prophets (Hos. 3:4-5), John preached that the sincerity of that external act implied more, namely the *need for interior repentance* or remorse for the sin. John's form of baptism was thus preparatory and provisional, a "preview" of Christian baptism, which would complete John's form of baptism by adding an element of faith in the very person removing the sin, Jesus the Redeemer. John's baptism emphasized the acknowledgment of one's human sinfulness, and thus created a sense of need for what was to be specifically revealed later, namely, that Jesus' death would bring about the forgiveness of sin.

This explains why Apollos, even while preaching Jesus' doctrine, "knew *only* the baptism of John" (Acts 18:25), until Priscilla and Aquila "explained to him the way of God *more adequately*" (v. 26).

Apollos knew something about Jesus, but basically, he, like John, was still looking forward to the coming of the Messiah, so his baptism was not in the name of Jesus, but was based on repentance rather than on the completing element of repentance, namely faith in Jesus as Redeemer.

Likewise, when Paul discovered that the twelve Ephesian disciples had received only John's baptism, he explained, "John's baptism was a baptism of repentance. John told the people to believe in the one coming *after* him, that is, Jesus. On hearing this, they were baptized in the name of the Lord Jesus" (Acts 19:4-5). John's baptism, because it was merely a historical precedent, could be called "inadequate"; it was meant to create an anticipation for Christian baptism the way a preview of a movie is designed to create a desire to see the movie itself.

Parenthetically, to solve an interdenominational controversy, the baptism "in the name of Jesus" is not a contradiction of Jesus' command to baptize in the Trinitarian formula (Mt. 28:19). The phrase "in the name of Jesus" emphasizes the characteristic of Christian baptism effective because of Jesus' redemptive act, as distinguished from John's repentance-baptism that lacked that faith-in-Jesus element.

Once a person was "born again of water" — born into a new life as a child of God, and member of Christ's mystical body, he or she needed to grow quickly into spiritual adulthood with "adult power" — that is, born again of the Spirit, endued with the Spirit's life and *power* so as to effectively evangelize others, building up the Kingdom of God (Acts 1:8).

How often should a Catholic receive the sacrament of reconciliation and the Holy Eucharist?

Consideration of the "Easter duty" sheds light on the very *minimum* obligation concerning Communion and confession. The Easter duty refers only to the obligation of annual Communion; there is, strictly speaking, no confession obligation, even annually, for someone with only venial sins committed since the last worthy confession.

116

This is the minimum *canonical* obligation. But the minimum is not enough to deal with one's *spiritual* needs adequately, as Pope John Paul II pointed out. The richness of a grace-filled sacramental life would be lacking. If a Catholic receives Communion only annually, or confesses only annually, that person can hardly be called a "good" Catholic, even if he or she attends Mass every week. The Church encourages at least monthly confession for laity and twice-monthly confession for clergy and religious, and of course Communion at least weekly, preferably even daily.

Is it possible, as St. Paul suggests in his letter to the Corinthians, that the living can be baptized again for the dead?

The passage which refers to this matter is I Cor. 15:29, where Paul writes, "If there is no resurrection (of our bodies), what will those do who are baptized for the dead? If the dead are not raised at all, why are people baptized for them?"

The use of the present tense indicates that this was a custom current at the time of Paul in Corinth. But he mentions this custom almost in passing, as one of his arguments to substantiate the doctrine of the resurrection of the dead that we state in the Apostles' Creed and the Nicene Creed. Paul neither approves nor disapproves of the practice of baptism for the dead, in this passage or anywhere else. But the practice was evoked to substantiate the doctrine of the resurrection of the body, which is mentioned in many places in the Gospels and epistles, as well as Old Testament references like Job 19:25-27. Many attempts have been made through the centuries to explain Paul's remark about baptism for the dead. I'll present here four of the most plausible explanations, none of which would warrant one's undergoing a baptismal service in the name of a deceased person, after the fashion of the Mormon practice.

1) Paul could have been referring to the fact that new

converts were being baptized to fill the ranks of Christians who had died, thus sharing with them in the Christian status when resurrected, and to keep alive among the living Christians the fundamental doctrine about the bodily resurrection on the last day.

2) Paul could have been pointing out that it was mainly in anticipation of the resurrection of the *dead* that Christians were being baptized, since baptism symbolizes a spiritual resurrection (Col. 2:12) analogous to the physical resurrection.

3) Paul may have been saying that believers who had died with only baptism of desire, not having completed the preparation for water baptism, could be "baptized" vicariously by their loved ones in a *non-sacramental* way somewhat similar to "devotional" symbolic "baptism" engaged in by anyone blessing himself with holy water, or by renewing baptismal promises in the Holy Saturday liturgy, or by being submerged in the River Jordan as a devotional act reminiscent of baptism. Such non-sacramental rituals would then merely serve the purpose of a pious expression of the living relative's desire or wish that the dead person would have been able to receive water baptism.

4) A fourth possible explanation (which I think is the most cogent) is that through the entire paragraph Paul shows that the bodily resurrection of believers in the end time is guaranteed by the bodily resurrection of Christ himself. In this context Paul alludes to the custom of dying Christians urging unconverted relatives around their deathbed to get right with God, who is accessible only through the resurrected Christ (Jn. 14:6). Deeply moved by this admonition, many unconverted relatives would come to believe and be baptized as Jesus commanded (Mk. 16:16). When the dying person was finally dead, it was for that person's sake (*"for the sake of the dead"*) that the non-believer was converted and baptized, even though the primary motive was to get right with God.

The early Christians understood that faith cannot be imputed from one person to another, just as contrition cannot be had for another person, nor could one person undergo baptism for another, living or dead. But one who had been deeply moved by the testimony of a dying believer may easily be moved to join him in faith, repentance, and commitment to the Lord — in the joyous expectation of meeting that loved one later in his glorified resurrected body.

In effect, then, according to this fourth opinion, what Paul is saying is: "What shall they do who are baptized for the sake of the dead? If dead people are not really raised up, why are they baptized for their sake?" Continuing this theme in the next verse (1 Cor. 15:30), he asks, "As for us, why do we endanger ourselves every hour?" In verse 32 he concludes (quoting Isaiah 22:13), "If the dead are not raised [bodily from their graves], then 'let us eat and drink, for tomorrow we [too] die.' " In other words, if hope of bodily resurrection is a delusion, then Christ himself could not have risen bodily, and hence the entire Gospel is a fraud, and there is no deliverance from sin and hell. "If Christ has not been raised, your faith is futile; you are still in your sins. Then those also who have fallen asleep in Christ are lost" (vss. 17-18).

There is no conversion by proxy, just as there is no baptism by proxy. Such a teaching cannot be found anyplace in Scripture, so being baptized for any deceased person is out of the question. But one of the above four explanations may be expected to explain the problematic passage. I feel quite certain that the last explanation is the best, by far.

Haven't all baptized Christians already received a "baptism in the Holy Spirit"?

All four Gospels say that there is a difference between "water baptism" and "baptism in the Holy Spirit," with John the Baptist emphasizing that distinction: "I baptize you with water, but he [Jesus] will baptize you with the Holy Spirit" (Mk. 1:8; see Mt. 3:11; Lk. 3:16; Jn. 1:33).

119

Dissenting theologians claim that it was the Church that corporately received the Holy Spirit at Pentecost, and all Christians partake of that general outpouring — somewhat like a huge vat being water-filled, with many spigots for individuals to draw from the general supply. In this view, the baptism in the Spirit is not an additional experience subsequent to becoming a Christian, but a privilege that everyone experiences by simply being a Christian and thus partaking of the fullness of the Spirit-presence in the Church from the time of water-baptism. If this partaking can be called charismatic, then of course every Christian would be charismatic from the moment of Christian initiation by water baptism.

However, this theological theory is debunked by St. Thomas Aquinas, who shows that within an individual there is a distinction between the *"indwelling"* of the Spirit (occasioned by water baptism or Christian initiation) and the *"infilling"* of the Spirit (occasioned by a pentecostal experience of being baptized in the Spirit).

Jesus also makes the distinction, in a pre-Pentecost discourse with his disciples in John 14:17, by using two separate prepositions: "with" and "in": "The Spirit . . . lives with you [now] and will be in you [later]." There are obviously two different levels of intimacy by which the Spirit can relate to an individual.

The baptisms mentioned in Hebrews 6:2 were referred to by Jesus at the beginning of his public life: in John 3:5 he tells Nicodemus that a person must be "born of water and the Spirit." Again, at the very end of his earthly existence, just before his Ascension, Jesus distinguishes between the two baptisms: "John baptized with water, but in a few days you will be baptized with the Holy Spirit" (Acts 1:5).

The disciples were already Christians, of course, since they had already received spiritual life for having heard his word and believed in the one who sent him (Jn 5:24); and Jesus had assured them that they were "clean" (13:10), with their names "recorded in heaven" (Lk. 10:20). Furthermore, the resurrected Jesus had breathed upon them, even imparting the Holy Spirit to activate a ministerial gift of forgiving sins (Jn. 20:22-23). Yet he told them to wait for, and pray for, a subsequent (and therefore separate) grace of the baptism in the Spirit a "few days" later (see also Lk. 24:49) — clearly an additional experience beyond the basic Christianity they were already experiencing.

A close study of the Acts of the Apostles shows that the early Christians regarded it as normal and normative for believers to be baptized in the Holy Spirit; that is, a pre-charismatic Christian was regarded as a kind of "sub-normal" Christian. For instance, the Samaritans, mentioned in Acts 8, had fulfilled the two requirements for salvation given by Jesus (Mk. 16:16): belief and baptism. Yet, when Peter and John arrived in Samaria, they "prayed for them that they might receive the Holy Spirit, because the Holy Spirit had not yet come upon any of them; they had simply been baptized in the name of the Lord Jesus" (Acts 8:15-16). They obviously had not received the baptism of the Spirit at the time of their conversion and water baptism.

A similar example is seen in Acts 19. Paul found twelve disciples at Ephesus who were believers, and asked them, "Did you receive the Holy Spirit when (or after) you believed?" When they answered in the negative, Paul baptized them. Then, "when Paul placed his hands on them, the Holy Spirit came upon them, and they spoke in tongues and prophesied" (vs. 6). If mere believing or being converted automatically carried with it the baptism in the Spirit, then Paul's question would have been meaningless. The Ephesians' baptism in the Holy Spirit was subsequent to (and therefore distinct from) their belief in Christ and also their water baptism.

What is the so-called "baptism in the Holy Spirit" which charismatics talk about?

It's best to begin by explaining three separate states: 1) that of a baptized Christian in the state of grace, who is sacramentally and canonically a Christian, "baptized into union with Christ" (Gal. 3:27); 2) that of a "born-again" ("regenerated") Christian — one who has undergone a kind of "conversion" or "*metanoia*" experience, as the Greek Fathers called it, which involves a knowledge of and commitment to Jesus as one's Lord and personal Savior (see Gal. 2:20) — a state which Pope John Paul II said is lacking in many "sacramentalized" Christians; and 3) that of a charismatic Christian who has received the baptism in the Spirit as an experience separate from, and usually subsequent to, a "conversion" experience (see Titus 3:4-5).

Each of these three spiritual states can be lost or diminished in some way: the first, by mortal sin (see 1 Jn. 5:16-17); the second, by loss or diminution of an abiding commitment to Jesus as Lord (see Jn. 15:6); and the third, by not "living by the Spirit" (see Gal. 5:16-26).

This threefold distinction can be reduced to a twofold one to simplify my response, namely, the uncompromising distinction between a "pre-charismatic" Christian and a charismatic Christian — a distinction that seems to needle many non-charismatics, and raises the hackles of some theologians (whom I love to challenge).

The Pentecost experience of becoming charismatic by being "baptized in the Spirit" (Acts 1:5) is something clearly distinct from and beyond the experience of becoming a Christian by being "baptized into Christ" (Rom. 6:3) by water. The two baptisms have totally different purposes. Water baptism makes one a child of God in a special way, grafting one into the body of Christ (Gal. 3:27; Rom. 6:3), while Spirit baptism gives one charismatic power to be an effective witness (evangelizer) in building the Kingdom (Acts 1:8; Lk. 24:48-49).

122

While the baptism in the Spirit is always distinct from the conversion experience, it may not necessarily be subsequent to it, as in the case of Cornelius's household, who received the baptism in the Spirit before they were baptized in water (Acts 10:44-48). In recounting this episode at the Council of Jerusalem (Acts 15:7-9), Peter referred to separate acts: 1) purifying their hearts by faith (conversion), and 2) the gift of the Holy Spirit.

Paul's baptism in the Spirit at the hands of Ananias came three days after his conversion on the road to Damascus, and just before his water baptism (Acts 9:3-18). Here again, the baptism of the Spirit is seen as a distinct experience.

It should be noted that the baptism in the Spirit ought not to be a one-time, isolated event, but should be the beginning of a "growth in the Spirit," with "refilling" periodically (by prayer meetings, etc.). That is why the author of Hebrews says, "Let us not give up meeting together, as some are in the habit of doing" (Heb. 10:25). Notice that when Peter and John joined their friends in a prayer meeting after being released from prison, they were again filled with the Holy Spirit (Acts 4:31). The exact translation of Ephesians 5:18 is not "Be filled with the Spirit" but "Begin *being* filled with the Holy Spirit" — an ongoing act. I could thus have all of the Holy Spirit without him having all of me.

What is a sacramental?

It is a sign of grace instituted within the Church, without the solemnly sacred, necessary character of a sign instituted by Christ.

In the case of all sacramentals, the power comes not from the sign itself, but by means of the Church's official (liturgical, not private) prayer of blessing — a power the Church derives from Christ himself (see Mt. 16:19, 18:18). As the Vatican II document on the Liturgy states (*Sacrosanctum Concilium*, art.

123

61), both sacraments and sacramentals sanctify us, not of themselves, but by the power flowing from the redemptive act of Jesus, elicited by the Church's intercession to be directed through those external signs and elements. Hence sacramentals like blessed salt, holy water, medals, etc. are not to be used superstitiously as having self-contained power, but as a "focus-point" funneling one's faith toward Jesus, just as a flag is used as a "focus-point" of patriotism, or as handkerchiefs were used to focus faith for healing and deliverance by Paul (Acts 19:12).

Vatican II urges us to participate *"intelligently and actively"* in the use of sacramentals, just as in the use of sacraments.

As with the use of sacraments, much depends on the faith and devotion of the person using blessed salt or any sacramental. This faith must be Jesus-centered, as was the faith of the blind man in John 9; he had faith in Jesus, not in the mud and spittle used by Jesus to heal him.

In light of this, we can see why Vatican II states that "there is hardly any *proper* use of material things which cannot thus be directed toward the sanctification of persons and the praise of God" (art. 61 of Liturgy document). Hence new sacramentals may also be added when rituals are revised (art. 79).

Could you explain the origin and use of salt as a sacramental?

There is a renewed interest today in the ancient sacramental of blessed salt, especially by charismatics, in healing and deliverance situations, etc. To understand its proper use and its efficacy, it would be helpful to review the scriptural symbolism and its history.

Salt in the ancient world was a precious commodity (even monopolized by the royalty in Egypt and Persia). Roman soldiers were partially paid with packets of salt ("*sal*" in Latin); this was the origin of our word "*salary*" and of phrases like, "worth his salt," etc. Being costly, it was an appropriate offering to God as a "covenant of salt" (Lev. 2:13; 2 Chron. 13:5; Num. 18:19) used in sacrifices by the Israelites (Ezek. 43:24) and for the accompanying sacrificial meal (Gen. 31:54).

Belief in its preservative and healing properties led to its use to dry and harden the skin of newborns (Ezek. 16:4) and to prevent umbilical-cord infection. Used to preserve meats from deterioration, it became a symbol of preservation and spiritual incorruptibility that was to characterize anyone offering sacrificial worship. Shared at the sacrificial meal, salt became a symbol of friendship and hospitality, a custom-symbol still used today in Arab culture. Jesus referred to this salt-symbolized friendship covenant in Mark 9:50: "Have salt in yourselves and be at peace with one another" — that is, "preserve that quality (flavor) that makes you a blessing to one another." Note the double symbol of preservation and flavoring.

This double primary symbolization is also found in Paul's advice in Col. 4:6: "Let your conversation be always full of grace, seasoned with salt." That is, let it be wholesome and savory, preserved from the corrupting conversation of worldlings (3:8 and Eph. 4:29). (His use of the word salt may also have referred to another of its symbols: spiritual wisdom, since the Latin word for savor or taste, "*sapientia*," is the same as for wisdom.)

Some or all of these symbols may have been implied in Jesus' words to his chosen ones, describing them as the "salt of the earth" (Mt. 5:13). He especially indicated that they were to oppose the world's corruption, reminding them that as salt must preserve its own anti-corruptive quality, they too must preserve their anti-corruptive influence in a sin-corrupted world (see Lk. 14:34).

The blessing promised by God on food and water, as well as the prevention of miscarriages and agricultural catastrophes (Ex. 23:25-26) was extended by God through Elisha in Jericho

(2 Kings 2:20-21), when he was inspired to put salt into the contaminated water. Adding salt to already brackish water to decontaminate it made the miracle all the more impressive, since one would expect the opposite effect. This first miracle of Elisha is the primary scriptural basis for the sacramental use of blessed salt today, as the Roman Ritual indicates.

As a Catholic sacramental, salt blessed by the liturgical prayer of a priest may be used by itself, unmixed, as in exorcisms, and formerly in the exorcist prayer at baptism, or it may be mixed with water to make holy water, as the ritual prescribes (reminiscent of Elisha's miracle). In whichever form, it is intended to be an instrument of grace to preserve one from the corruption of evil occurring as sin, sickness, demonic influence, etc.

Thus used non-superstitiously, modest amounts of salt may be sprinkled in one's bedroom, or across thresholds to prevent burglary, in cars for safety, etc. A few grains in drinking water or used in cooking or as food seasoning often bring astonishing spiritual and physical benefits, as I have personally witnessed many times.

Any amount of salt may be presented to a priest for his blessing, using the following official prayer from the Roman Ritual:

"Almighty God, we ask you to bless this salt, as once you blessed the salt scattered over the water by the prophet Elisha. Wherever this salt (and water) is sprinkled, drive away the power of evil, and protect us always by the presence of your Holy Spirit. Grant this through Christ our Lord. Amen."

Sin

Isn't it unjust for God to allow all people to suffer from the original sin of our first parents, Adam and Eve?

God did impose a tremendous responsibility on our first parents, Adam and Eve, as the progenitors of the human race, and they clearly knew the consequences of their sin before they sinned (Gen. 2:17). Therefore it was not unjust of God to punish them and their offspring; rather it was unjust of them to so seriously offend the infinite majesty of God. Moreover, not leaving mankind spiritually deprived, God promised a Redeemer to open the gates of heaven closed by original sin. Hence, St. Augustine calls the first sin a "*felix culpa*" — a "happy fault." In this we see the "good from evil" principle that manifests God's tremendous goodness.

Why must people suffer for sins when Christ has already died to redeem us?

The redemption remitted guilt, not punishment for sin. The redeemed suffer, yet not *all* suffering is punishment for sins, as Jesus said (Jn. 9:3), and when suffering is related to our sin, it is more often a form of discipline than a punishment, as it says in Hebrews 12:7-11.

Paul reminds us that "nothing you do *for the Lord* is ever wasted" (1 Cor. 15:58 LB); yet much suffering is wasted by many people through not accepting it "for the Lord." They waste their suffering by complaining and by resisting God's permissive will that allows suffering. It requires consummate faith to surrender undeviatingly to the mystery of God's love expressed in unavoidable suffering. When suffering, one might well pray for the grace to live the words of Scripture: "We *believe* him when he tells us that he loves us dearly" (1 Jn. 4:16 LB).

Jesus reminds us that hoping to escape suffering in this life is futile (Jn. 16:33). But his holy word also reminds us that sanctified suffering is not without its hundredfold reward. In the anguish of our tribulations, let us not try to water down the fundamental truth affirmed by Paul and Barnabas as they emerged from their trials: "We must go through many hardships to enter the kingdom of God" (Acts 14:22).

What is meant by "cooperating in another's sin"?

Some old catechisms listed nine ways of sharing another's guilt, but surprisingly they omitted the most frequent one, namely, bad example. The "classical" listing of ways of sharing guilt included the following: By advice, by command, by consent, by provocation, by praise or flattery, by concealment, by being a partner in the sin, by silence, and by defending the evil done.

But first, a word about bad example, omitted from the "classical" list of cooperative sins. Bad example is often not recognized as sin, though it may be quite serious. It could include positive sins like unwholesome peer pressure, parental bad example, etc., or negative sins of omission (Jas. 4:17), like neglect of parental obligations regarding proper sex education, neglect of religious training (see Prov. 22:6, 29:15), neglecting church attendance (Heb. 10:25) or home prayer (Is. 38:19). Consider the far-reaching effects of David's failure to restrain his son Adonijah (1 Kings 1:6), or the prolonged punishment from God for Eli's neglect to restrain his sons (1 Sam. 3:13).

To recognize the extent of bad example, notice the common statistic that three out of four children of divorced parents will end their own marriages in divorce. Sixty-five percent of drug- or alcohol-dependent youths have at least one parent who is also hooked. Proverbs 19:18 warns, "Be not a party to your son's [spiritual] death" (see also 22:15 and 23:14). Jesus used fiery words to excoriate those who scandalize "these little ones": "things that cause others to sin are bound to come, but woe to that person by whom they come" (Lk. 17:1; Mt. 18:7). (For a deeper look at this serious matter, see my booklet, "The Poison of Bad Example.")

Let us now consider the catechism list of cooperative sins, with examples of each, to show how multifarious they are in our society today.

1) Sinning by counsel (advice). This is sinful persuasion, referred to in the Bible as "the counsel of the wicked" (Ps. 1:1). Today it is common among doctors, counselors, parents, and partners in encouraging abortion, or young people enticing their peers to try drugs. Telling a youngster to lie about his age to get reduced travel fare or admission fees, or teaching Catholic students that neglecting the Sunday Mass obligation isn't a serious matter — all would be examples of this. Also most Planned Parenthood counseling, or any advice that would knowingly lead others astray (see Mk. 13:22; 1 Tim. 4:1; 2 Tim. 3:13, etc.).

2) Sinning by command. Examples would include: the Iraqi authorities commanding attacks on noncombatants, or commanding the torching of oil wells or spilling oil in the Persian Gulf as needless and spiteful environmental devastation; military atrocities against civilians, from Vietnam to El Salvador; Herod's commanding the soldiers to slaughter the innocents; one spouse demanding that the other be sterilized or practice artificial birth control; requiring an accountant to juggle financial accounts unjustly; keeping one's child from Mass or from receiving the sacraments, or from visiting a divorced parent (where there's no moral or physical danger); demanding that an employee commit perjury or repress information about industrial waste, abuses, etc.

3) Sinning by consent, as Paul (then Saul) did in holding the garments of those stoning Stephen to death. Consent can be

by participation also, in things like seances, fortune-telling, neglecting to strive to prevent invalid marriages of one's children; by not protesting unethical business practices in one's company, by providing alcohol to an alcoholic, by not showing displeasure at blasphemy or gossip, etc.

4) Sinning by provocation, like the crowd at Jesus' crucifixion shouting, "Crucify him!" "Stirring up dissension is detestable to the Lord" (Prov. 6:19, 6:14). Other examples: seduction, as in prostitution; enticing someone to reveal gossip; encouraging suicide or euthanasia; inviting one to become a gang member; maliciously leading one away from religious convictions (see Acts 20:30); producing, displaying, or sharing pornography; drawing someone into an argument or fight; causing strife or disharmony (Eph. 4:31) among fellow workers, prayer-group members, etc. "He who loves a quarrel loves sin," says Proverbs 17:19; "Starting a quarrel is like breaching a dam" (v. 14). Many a divorce had its start in spouses nagging or provoking one another to anger. "The Lord's servant must not quarrel," warns Paul (2 Tim. 2:24).

After describing sins of homosexuality, depravity, envy, murder, etc., Paul asserts that evil persons not only do these things, but also sin by provocation in approving others practicing such sins (Rom. 1:32). In Mafia brotherhoods, political graft conspiracies, occultic group recruitment, industrial price-fixing consortiums, etc. such provocation is blatantly common, but also in gay communities, so-called "escort services," etc. Paul writes, "In this matter [of sexual immorality] no one should wrong his brother or take advantage of him. The Lord will punish men for all such sins" (1 Thess. 4:6).

5) Sinning by praise or flattery, like those who flattered King Darius into arrogating divinity to himself (Dan. 6:7). Extolling a cult leader or guru as superhuman, as the throngs did with Herod (Acts 12:22); complimenting someone on a shady business deal or tax-evasion; "apple-polishing" an unworthy political candidate, or succumbing to majority jury

pressure to get an unjust legal decision (see Prov. 24:24) would be forms of this kind of cooperative sin. Parents favoring one of their children over another could indirectly fail in this way.

6) Sinning by concealment, like Saul promising secrecy to the witch of Endor to protect her from prosecution (1 Sam. 28:10). One could sin in this way by harboring criminals, concealing criminal evidence from the court, by not reporting a crime, by refusing to give testimony as a witness to an accident or crime, by distorting reports to help another pad an expense account, a doctor by falsifying medical reports for insurance claims, by hiding goods stolen by another, by paying a worker in cash to help him conceal taxable income, by distorting truth in a letter of recommendation, being undeservedly on welfare, by participating in an election fraud, etc. "He who conceals sin does not prosper," warns Solomon (Prov. 28:13).

7) Sinning by being a partner in sin. Many sins are conspiratorial, such as kickbacks and bribery common in the business world (see Mic. 7:3). Other forms of "partner sin" include invalid marriages, adultery, fornication, homosexuality (the act, not the orientation itself); hired killers, abortionists with the patients seeking abortions, team robberies, gang warfare, gang rape, drug traffickers and users, etc. Almost every marital conflict involves partnership in sin by mutual anger, resentment, refusal to foster marital love and hence matrimonial grace (Eph. 5:26). The list is endless.

8) Sinning by silence. "The wicked person does not reject what is wrong" (Ps. 36:4). Sinning by silence is often similar to sinning by concealment, mentioned above. A parent neglecting to correct a wayward child would sin by silence. Not reporting sexual harassment in an office, or ongoing scandal by a clergyman, would be to participate in the sin of the culprit. A political leader who ignores needs affecting the common welfare would likewise sin by silence, as would anyone neglecting the obligation to correct a subordinate for whom one is responsible.

9) Sinning by defending evil. An example: defending a

violator of human rights. A criminal lawyer defending the *rights* of a criminal must not defend the guilt itself. Supporting a pro-abortion candidate *because* of that issue would be sinful, even though the candidate may be subjectively innocent by his sincerity (Rom. 2:15; 1 Cor. 4:5).

The Bible provides the antidote to cooperative evil in the form of cooperative love: "Whoever loves his brethren lives in the light, and there is nothing in him to make him stumble" (1 Jn. 2:10).

Since observing the "Lord's Day" relates to our relationship with God, isn't disregard of Sabbath obligations very sinful?

In Exodus 31:15-17 God commanded that every seventh day (Sabbath) be a workless day, patterned after the Lord's "rest" after his "six" days of creation. Twice in that chapter God demands the death penalty for violators of this ordinance: would you insist this penalty be applied along with the Sabbath ordinance as an equally unchangeable command of God? I doubt that any modern Jew, no matter how orthodox, would seek the death penalty for anyone working on the Sabbath. Yet that's the clear command of God, twice affirmed. Obviously it is assumed that a secondary part of the law — the penalty factor — could be changed without essentially affecting the basic law.

Each of the Ten Commandments represents a facet of the natural law expressing an ethical intuition of human nature, which is unchangeable. Thus there is a general unchangeable obligation by natural law for humans to worship God. Yet some particular specifics in the formulation of that norm are not intrinsic to the natural law, such as the specific day or frequency required for worship of the Creator. Thus, the will of God is essentially fulfilled even when the specifics of the law are changed.

Yet even these specifics shouldn't be changed unless there is some basis in divine revelation for doing so. But there is a basis in revelation for a secondary change in the law to "keep holy the Sabbath" where the natural law was not affected, just as there was in the suspension of the dietary (kosher) laws (Acts 10:15; I Tim. 4:3-4). With this qualification, Paul could write that "you are not under law, but under grace" (Rom. 6:14-15).

By the time of Christ, the interpretation of the Sabbath injunction was such that Jesus himself often made exception to the Sabbath law (Mt. 12:1-12; Lk. 13:10-17; Jn. 5:9, 16) and established it with a new emphasis as a day on which one could work by helping his fellow humans (Mk. 2:23-28; 3:4).

Jesus, who called himself "the Lord of the Sabbath" (Mt. 12:8), thus intimated that the most rigid application of the law in this matter of the Sabbath was not always in accord with God's will, reminding the Pharisees that "on the Sabbath even the priests in the temple desecrate the day (doing temple work) and yet are innocent" (vs. 5). If the work of circumcision is allowed on the Sabbath, he argued, why not the work of healing? "Stop judging by mere appearance, and make a right judgment," he insisted (Jn. 7:23-24). That's still good advice today for Sabbath-law literalists.

Virtues and Vice

Doesn't buying insurance reflect a lack of trust in God's providential care?

Faith and trust in God does not assure us of a problem-free, accident-free life. When a working family member dies or is disabled, insurance can provide for the family's support — itself a biblical mandate: "If anyone does not provide for his relatives, and especially for his immediate family, he . . . is worse than an unbeliever" (I Tim. 5:8). Health insurance can be a form of charity by preventing a family from falling into economic straits, through the subsidizing of medical payments.

Insurance provides a kind of pool of invested resources from which the participants share the financial burdens of one another as required. It is true that insurance is a form of gambling (betting the insurance company that you will suffer loss of life, health or material possessions, against their wager that you won't). But gambling is not *intrinsically* evil (though circumstances can make it evil), as shown in another question in this book dealing with that subject.

Liability insurance is a way of compensating someone who has suffered loss because of another's action or negligence. That, too, finds a basis in Scripture (Ex. 21:22). Neglecting liability insurance could leave one open to bankruptcy that would deprive one's creditors, or it could result in the injustice of an accident victim being left without compensation. Of course prudence should be used in deciding the kinds and amount of insurance one should carry, keeping in mind legal requirements and also one's ability to afford the insurance.

Putting the entire insurance question into the framework of the active and passive phases of God's will, it becomes clear that refusing to be insured so as to neglect one's family's security — aside from a special well-discerned inspiration to do so — would not normally fit into the passive ("good-pleasure") will of God. In fact, in *most* cases, being insured would more properly fit in the category of God's active ("signified") will — things he wants us to do. Thus, it is not a sign of trust in God, but rather a rash "tempting" of God to refuse to be insured. This norm certainly allows for exceptions, as in the case of a well-discerned inspiration to the contrary by God's sovereign choice.

Being insured does not contravene Jesus' mandate to avoid worry by trusting in his protective providence (Mt. 6:25-34), because his protective providence often works instrumentally through human agencies such as modern technology, the medical profession, the judicial system, and even insurance companies (in spite of their obvious inequities and iniquities).

What is meant by the virtue of trust?

Total surrender to God in holy trust is a beautiful virtue, and the most "passive" of all fifty-six virtues, but it is also one of the most misunderstood virtues. Trust in God, or "holy abandonment" is not meant to be *totally* passive — no virtue is, as Pope Pius XI said. Otherwise, to practice it would be to succumb to the heresy of Quietism, which sought the extinction of the human will — as proposed by the seventeenth-century Spanish priest Molinos.

There's an old bromide, which had its origin in maritime emergencies, that says, "Pray, sailor, but row for shore." A better-known aphorism is "God helps those who help themselves." Embodied in those homey platitudes is some substantial theology that touches on your question.

Moses, with the Pharaoh in hot pursuit, mistakenly told the Israelites that they needed only to stand still and be passive, saying that the Lord would fight for them. But "The Lord said to Moses, 'Why are you crying out to me? Tell the Israelites to move forward!' " (Ex. 14:15). Only then did God part the sea at Moses' command. Likewise, Peter could never have walked on water by God's power if he hadn't actively initiated the miracle by stepping out of the boat at Jesus' invitation (Mt. 14:29). God wants to help us, but he expects our cooperation. It is foolish to pray for a job but refuse to go job-hunting, and equally rash to refuse medical attention while waiting for a miraculous healing (unless *clearly* inspired by God to do so).

Thirteenth-century theology distinguished between God's conditional and non-conditional will. God's conditional will has an "if" involved; thus he wills your health, *if* you take care of it, *if* you pray enough for healing, *if* you pray with deep faith, etc. His non-conditional will can be either his permissive will (things he reluctantly allows, like war, burglary, rape, murder, etc.) or his positive will — things he positively desires. This positive will can in turn be his active "signified will" (things God wants us to do, like eat, sleep, go to church, pay our debts, avoid sin, etc.), or his passive "good-pleasure will" (things God wants to happen to us, like good or bad weather, accidents, mosquito bites, slow-up from traffic jams, being loved and accepted by others or misunderstood by them, etc.).

Any situation in life fits into one of these categories of God's will. Grasping these distinctions can help you understand and conform to God's will, by properly reacting to eventualities in life, or preventing them, in some cases.

Is gambling evil or wrong?

The answer to your question is more complicated than you might imagine. It is right to say that gambling is not *intrinsically* evil (though it can become intrinsically evil by fostering gambling addiction, by impoverishing one's family, by supporting organized crime, by fostering greed, materialism, etc.). Taking out an insurance policy or insuring a mailed package is a form of gambling; so is paying for an extended service warranty on a household appliance. Hence, it's obvious that not all gambling is sinful.

But your question touches on a more subtle point — God's will in gambling. Paul speaks of three "levels" of God's will: "good, pleasing, and perfect" in reference to "not conforming to the pattern of this world" (Rom. 12:2). "Good" means not bad (no evil intent); "pleasing" means striving to please God; "perfect" means earnestly wanting God's will to be done perfectly "on earth as it is in heaven." Obviously your question doesn't lend itself to an "either-or" answer. It may involve more than the use of common sense; it may involve the grace-driven virtue of prudence (Prov. 1:3, 13:16, 14:8, 15, 18), or beyond that, the Holy Spirit's gift of counsel (Ps. 73:24; 1 Kings 22:5; 2 Chr. 18:4, etc.).

But lest this answer become overcomplicated, let's put Paul's triple division into an existential context. You would certainly be in the "good" will of God if you excluded all evil intent such as greed, by wanting to win the lottery for your necessities, not luxuries. To want to give all the proceeds to the poor would go further and be "pleasing" to God. But would the lottery ticket purchase be within the "perfect" will of God? This third level might be difficult to determine unless one was extremely mature spiritually and had the gift of counsel (Is. 11:2), which would provide overwhelming spiritual intuition about God's will in given circumstances. In persons less mature, operating on the prudential level (grace-impelled but not inspired), simple data would be helpful in making the decision about gambling. The following are examples of such data that circumspect persons might consider with regard to a lottery:

You have a greater chance of being struck by lightning than of winning a million-dollar jackpot from an average state lottery (one chance in 14 million!). Good purposes are often frustrated: California's $600 million income for public education from the lottery was offset by that same amount dropped from state funding. Lotteries provide less than two percent of state revenue, and the lottery has lowered no one's taxes as yet. The lottery creates very few jobs, low paying ones at that, and lowers the amount of spendable income that would provide more work for others. Lotteries hurt the poor, who spend seven times as much as the rich on this form of gambling. Lotteries fuel compulsive gambling, which accounts for forty percent of the nation's white-collar crime (by embezzlement, etc.). A state lottery draws organized crime to compete with it by untaxed betting, sports betting, credit offers, etc.

Most gamblers find it hard to keep in mind that we are all really stewards of God's resources in some way, and we must render an account to him of how we handle his resources vis-à-vis his will. Undoubtedly there are casual gamblers who are able to avoid all the major pitfalls of gambling. For them it remains only to ascertain whether to gamble would fulfill the "good" will of God, the "pleasing" will of God, or the "perfect" will of God. That is seldom easy to determine.

INDEX

139

147

148